UNVEILED FACES

UNVEILED FACES:

Men and Women of the Bible

by

Mary Catherine Barron, C.S.J.

The Liturgical Press

Collegeville, Minnesota

Acknowledgments: Our gratitude to the editors of *Review for Religious* and *Sisters Today* for permission to reprint the following articles:

Review for Religious

"Prayer and the Desert" (November 1975)
"On Burying Our Isaacs" (September 1976)
"Of Symbols and Symbolists" (March 1979)
"In Process: John the Baptist" (July 1977)
"Running with Jonah: A Drama in Three Acts" (September 1978)
"Sitting It Out with Job: The Human Condition" (July 1979)

Sisters Today

"Pneumatic Fascination: The Elijah within Us" (January 1977)
"The Jonathan Time: On Reconciliation" (November 1977)
"A Journey Through Loneliness" (April 1979)
"Trysting with Love: Jacob's Wrestling" (May 1978)

Excerpts from the New American Bible, copyright © 1970, Confraternity of Christian Doctrine, Washington, D.C., and from The Jerusalem Bible, copyright © 1966 by Darton, Longman & Todd, Ltd. and Doubleday & Company, Inc. Used by permission.

Photos by Hugh Witzmann, O.S.B.

Library of Congress Cataloging in Publication Data

Barron, Mary Catherine, 1944–
    Unveiled Faces.

    1. Bible — Biography — Meditations.   I. Title.
BS571.B38   220.9'2   10-27728
    ISBN 0-8146-1212-1

To my mother
   Elizabeth MacEntee Barron
whose wit, vivacity, and way with words
enfleshes and inspirits this book

   and

To my father
   General Joseph William Barron, U.S.A.F.,
whose soaring visions and powerful love
is its heart.

    ***

"See! I make all things new" (Rev 21:5).

*the Torah
at the Western Wall
Jerusalem*

CONTENTS

FOREWORD

"And we, with our unveiled faces reflecting like mirrors the brightness of the Lord, all grow brighter and brighter as we are turned into the image that we reflect; this is the work of the Lord who is Spirit" (2 Cor 3:18).

This little volume, honed out over the years, is meant to be a mirror. It holds up for reflection various men and women of Scripture who struggled to image the brightness of the Lord. As with these biblical persons, so it is with us: outlines of the divine are often etched "through a glass darkly."

May this therefore be a book of encouragement. We are all weak human persons as were our spiritual ancestors. And we relate the same basic story, though differing in time and experience. It is a narrative of movement and conversion: grappling with the darkness, wrestling with the unknown, straining towards the light.

As we yearn and stretch for this Radiant Center, may all that shrouds our goodness drop as so many veils, leaving us transparent to the illumination of the Lord. And thus may we gradually come to image fully him whom we now partially reflect.

M.C.B.

Feast of Christ the King
November 23, 1980

9

Hagar

I had so little to call my own:
    a few small trinkets,
    a space to lie and think,
    the daily duties of my work,
    and all my tangled dreams.

So it was no outrage that torrid night
    of shifting desert sands,
    to feel his shadow lengthen over me.
Nor were there any words except his few:
    "Your mistress Sarai sent me."

Freedom has its own conditions—
    and I was bound.
And descendants, too numerous to be counted,
    cried out for satisfaction and an origin.
Thus he took me, according to their law.

A mighty desert prince, my thoughts had named
      him,
    Imperious, masterful, and free.
But who can know the desperate bonds of wedlock
    that chafe away the soul,
    save one who wears its chains?

Thus fettered, he enslaved me—
    with all his aching hopes,
    with the richness of his household,
    the cries of anxious Sarai,
    and the promise of his seed.

The rest is text, passion, wrenched and pained:
   jealousy, exile, and submission;
   the painful birth that yielded but a slave;
   the terrible choice that made one son no heir;
   and I, misused, rejected, then forgotten.

Since those years, the sun is all eclipse;
   the blazing stars of fortune have winked out;
   the croon of cradle-grave
     rocks fitful Sarai;
   and Abram nods towards death.

And yet, implacably, across the desert waste,
I sit, brood, ponder, listen, wait —
   and strain to catch a cadence on the wind
   of voice, and step, and touch that might yield
     him.
And long to know again the joy and doom,
   watching his shadow lengthen in my room.
   "Your mistress Sarai sent me."

On Burying Our Isaacs

The word of God is something alive and active: it cuts like any double-edged sword but more finely: it can slip through the place where the soul is divided from the spirit, or joints from the marrow; it can judge the secret emotions and thoughts. No created thing can hide from him; everything is uncovered and open to the eyes of the one to whom we must give an account of ourselves (Heb 4:12-13).

It happened some time later that God put Abraham to the test (Gen 22:1).

Abraham was a vulnerable man. He could never quite master the art of resisting God. Always, he was too available. Had he been a more pragmatic human being, he would have quickly cultivated a quality of deafness where God was concerned — or at least a fair pretense of it. But that was his weakness: he was too receptive. Whenever God called, he answered. Such alacrity can be dangerous, especially where Yahweh is involved. He is all-consuming.

And so when, after a short span of years of relative peace and quiet, God once again cried out his name: "Abraham, Abraham," our Old Testament forefather responded as could be expected: "Here I am." He should have known better. He should have realized the incipient danger of those words, because he had uttered them before and they had cost him quite a bit of pain. In fact, they had brought him to where he was then: in a strange land of strange people with a young son, the fruit of his and Sarah's old age. It had been a weary journey to this destination, filled with suffering and hope, alienation and promise, discouragement and fulfillment. But today, existence was peaceful and God was benign and Abraham was happy in the new life growing up around him: Isaac, his son. So he never should have answered with such openness, such literalness, when he said: "Here I am." Those three words capsulized a whole lifetime of givenness and surrender on Abraham's part and God knew that. He knew the implied depths of Abraham's response because long ago he had blasted his foundation, carved him out, and molded him in faith. So God was not surprised at Abraham's reply. He had tested him before.

Purgation is a messy business. No matter how finely wrought the instrument, there is always pain and a certain amount of blood-letting. Ironically, although we are quite familiar with the concept, we are never much at ease in the throes of the process. Double-edged swords are dangerous, especially the ones that slip into the hidden place "where the soul is divided from the spirit," because eventually they strike the heart. Abraham had been prodded and probed before. But he had also lived long enough to realize that there are always untouched recesses, crevices of the heart, where the finger of God has not yet been felt.

One of those crevices contained Isaac. And so Yahweh commands: "Take your son, your only child Isaac, whom you love, and go to the land of Moriah. There you shall offer him as a burnt offering, on a mountain I will point out to you" (Gen 22:2). God couldn't have been more blunt nor, apparently, more unfeeling. With near ferocity, he highlights the very nadir points involved in Abraham's sacrifice: "son," "only child," "Isaac," "whom you love." And then he conjures up a picture of that supple-limbed first fruit of endless expectation: blackened—a burnt offering on a wilderness mountaintop.

Abraham makes no response because he has already made the total one of "Here I am." We are simply told that early next morning he rises and begins the three days' journey to Moriah. Whatever the outcome, the journey itself is part of the purgation, is already a piece of the burnt offering, and the fact that it is leading to final consummation only intensifies the pain.

Anguish is not a very communicable emotion. It is too deep for utterance. So insistent is it that all other feelings give way before its flood. So Abraham says little on the pilgrimage to holocaust, but in grim irony loads Isaac with the wood and himself takes the knife and the fire. In stolid faith, Abraham bears in his own hands the purgative instruments that will cut and sear his son. But more deeply, he bears the instruments that will cut and sear *himself.* Isaac is to suffer a holocaust of body; Abraham suffers a holocaust of heart.

Outrage always accompanies the destruction of an innocent—outrage on the part of the nonparticipants. But who can fathom the outrage Abraham feels as he binds his only son and lays him on the altar? We cannot begin to plumb the depths of his grieving heart that still believes in the irrevocable word of Yahweh. "Abraham stretched out his hand and seized the knife to kill his son" (Gen 22:10).

Once again the cry comes: "Abraham, Abraham," and once again the familiar response is given: "I am here." And then come the salvific words: "Do not raise your hand against the boy; do not harm him, for now I know you fear God. You have not refused me your son, your only son" (Gen 22:11-13). Isaac is spared. What about Abraham? The holocaust of the body does not occur; the holocaust of the heart is complete.

We are accustomed to naming Abraham our "Father in Faith." Is he not also the "Father of Freed Love"? All the time he thought the journey was made to annihilate Isaac. Now he discovers that it was made to annihilate Abraham.

Father van Breemen in his book *Called By Name* offers the following analysis:

> When Abraham descends from the mountain with his son, both he and Isaac have changed; something has happened on that hilltop. . . . Like a tree which has been turned full circle in the ground, Abraham's roots have been cut loose, and he has returned a new man (p. 19).

In what does his newness consist? Abraham comes down the mountain with a living Isaac. Yet something in both of them is dead. Because he was bent over the prone Isaac on the altar, we could not see the pain in Abraham's eyes, the look of utter bewilderment at what he was about to do, the trembling terror at the death of love by his own hand. But Isaac could see. And in that look of love that was exchanged between them — father and son — the holocaust of the heart is accomplished. In that instant, Isaac cedes over his life to his father in trust and surrender. And Abraham cedes over his heart to Yahweh in a similar fashion. Because part of Abraham's heart *is* Isaac, that part of Isaac in Abraham's heart dies forever on Mount Moriah. Abraham returns to Beersheba with a son, but no longer with *his* son. Isaac is irrevocably gone, yielded over to Yahweh. Isaac returns with a father who is no longer solely *his* father, but more radically is father to Yahweh's people. Both lose and gain life; both surrender the other and are given the other in return — but transformed.

In the Letter to the Hebrews we are told:

> It was by faith that Abraham, when put to the test, offered up Isaac. He offered to sacrifice his only son even though the promises had been made to him and he had been told: It is through Isaac that your name will be carried on. He was confident that God had the power to raise the dead; and so, figuratively speaking, he was given back Isaac from the dead (Heb 11:17-19).

Centuries later, when speaking of losing and gaining life, Jesus would use the analogy of the wheat grain dying in the earth to produce a rich harvest. We might say that out of the seed of love for Isaac, which Abraham allows to die in the holy ground of Yahweh, comes the rich harvest of transformed life. For Abraham, indeed, has Isaac back from the dead, but only after he has first let him go. In a sense, he leaves Mount Moriah having buried part of himself and his son there.

So what does the story mean to us? Certainly we are relieved that Isaac is not slain. We are glad that Abraham's faith was vindicated. And we hope that we are never put to such a test. It is just such a latter mentality that is our mistake and our misfortune. For we all have our Isaacs — those hidden crevices of the heart where we do not even realize that "the soul is divided from the spirit." Unless we are willing to bury them (our Isaacs) in a holocaust of the heart, our faith is weak and our love is unfree. And to that extent we are poor spiritual progeny of our great desert patriarch.

The book of Judith tells us:

> We should be grateful to the Lord our God, for putting us to the test, as he did our forefathers. Recall how he dealt with Abraham, and how he tried Isaac, and all that happened to Jacob in Syrian Mesopotamia while he was tending the flocks of Laban, his mother's brother. Not for vengeance did the Lord put them in the crucible to try their hearts, nor has he done so with us. It is by way of admonition that he chastises those who are close to him (8:25-27).

Admonition for what? Admonition, so that eventually our hearts in the crucible will be so totally purified that we will, indeed, have laid to final rest all our Isaacs. Admonition, so that eventually our hearts in the crucible will be so totally free that we too will be able to respond as did Abraham to Yahweh's call: "Here I am."

"The word of God is something alive and active" — in Abraham's day and in our own. Will we let it pierce us, double-edged though it might be?

Rachelea

When all the pain and labor are finally done;
When all birth pangs are suffered, totaled, summed;
When all our anguish is your victory won;
Will it be worth it, Jacob,
    for a son?

Lea

No matter that you took me unaware;
Or that you love her better, with more care;
Or that my lot to plead and beg is scorned;
I am the one who gave you your first-born.

When all the pain and labor are finally done;
When all birth pangs are suffered, totaled, summed;
When all our anguish is your victory won;
Will it be worth it, Jacob,
    for a son?

Rachel

You loved me first and last and in between;
For me you hunger; for her, your love is lean;
And though each year she swells, I can attest
That my two children are your heart's bequest.

When all the pain and labor are finally done;
When all birth pangs are suffered, totaled, summed;
When all our anguish is your victory won;
Will it be worth it, Jacob,
    for a son?

Rachelea

How furtively we plot and vie and scheme;
How desperately we strive to meet the dream
    of many sons to take their father's name;
And what is left for us; what is our gain?

17

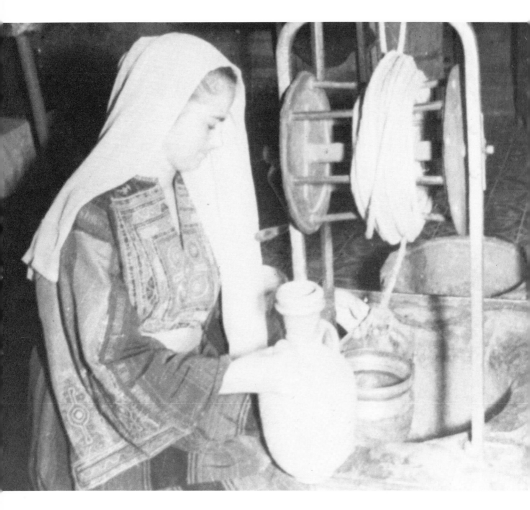

at Jacob's well
Shechem

When all the pain and labor are finally done;
When all birth pangs are suffered, totaled, summed;
When all our anguish is your victory won;
Will it be worth it, Jacob,
   for a son?

Rachelea   No matter, we are women; you, our lord,
You seed us, feed us, breed us — just reward.
And yet, some nights, the dark seduces question;
And achingly arouses with suggestion:

When all the pain and labor are finally done;
When all birth pangs are suffered, totaled, summed;
When all our anguish is your victory won;
Will they be worth it, Jacob,
   your twelve sons?

Trysting with Love: Jacob's Wrestling

Always he had grappled, even from the womb. Kicking, shoving, pushing, violently he had come forth, hand desperately extended, grabbing Esau's heel. And he was conniving, too, and cunning, and sly; ambitious to succeed no matter whose sockets snapped. Not altogether a likable fellow, this Jacob, although sole recipient of two women's jealous love. Not altogether a happy man, this patriarch, although sole administrator of vast lands and flocks and slaves.

He moved impatiently and scanned the silent sky. Today his emptiness stretched and yawned within him as wide and desolate as the endless desert sand. He was going home — *home* — with a retinue befitting an eastern prince or king. It spoke of a power and acquisition beyond even Isaac's misplaced blessing and of an earthly fulfillment transcending even Rebecca's wiles and schemes. And yet, so much was lacking.

He knew now, knew it as clearly and totally as he had known for years, that he would displace Esau; knew it as completely and achingly as he had felt Isaac die; knew it as breathlessly and heart-rendingly as he had first kissed Rachel; knew it as his constant loneliness and yearning.

What is a man to do with everything and nothing, riding across the desert waste with memories as his star? What rhythm does his heart make when it only pulsates pain? Beyond what horizon will there be a pause for peace?

A DECISION

He gave the word to halt, and groaning with a weariness no sleep could yet assuage, dismounted. He had made his decision. Esau would be foiled.

Can there be any enemy more treacherous than one's own brother? Is there any danger greater than love entrusted to one's kin? Jacob mused darkly and the bitterness of sparring years, wary days, and writhing hours numbed his heart. He knew what others thought of him in terms of hatred and of fear; how subtly respect edged itself with caution; how alien he was, even to himself.

How do the crisscross threads of life become so entangled? Why are there so many knots in the tapestry of years? He remembered never liking Esau, that wild hairy red-neck whose sole occupation consisted in eating what he killed. He remembered despising him for his easy satisfactions, his wild chases after game, his gruff blunt moments with their father. It was true, as neighbors claimed, Jacob was *Rebecca's* favorite, but somehow that only widened the chasm in his heart. Perhaps that was the reason now that he too chose a favorite and wielded with all others the chilling power called "withheld love." For years he had watched the agony trembling under Leah's smile, had felt the taut rivalry stretched between his wives, had heard the unvoiced clamorings from his sons who went unnoticed, had distanced himself irrevocably from any claims of love.

DISTRUST

He had come by it honestly — distrust. Rebecca had taught him early on that deception worked the best. It was true that she had helped him and that his interests were her own. And yet that day when he fled from Esau's violent rage, he knew he was also running from disillusionment in her. And as he ran he heard repeated in his heart, Isaac's anguished cry and Esau's choking plea:

> "Your brother came here by a ruse and carried off your blessing . . ." (Gen 27:35).
> "Father, bless me too . . ." (Gen 27:34).

He had thought that safe in Rachel he would regain himself, blot out those terrible moments that woke him from his sleep, purge from within his heart the bile that oozed from broken faith, and be healed. He did not realize how akin his uncle and his mother were nor how dark deceit can be when wrought upon oneself. So he had run to his marriage bed ecstatic at new life and had awakened in the dawn to find old times returned. It is true he still acquired Rachel in the end — every bit of her was his — and he possessed her daily with so urgent a rough love that under his intensity every caress was pain. He blamed himself that she had been so barren, not only of children but of vivacity and life. He remembered her that day she had come lithely to the well, when he had first kissed her and then had wept with joy. Those intervening years when he was bondsman for his bride had been the freest time Jacob had ever known. He never should have trusted in her father or his own heart. He should have known that love deceives you every time.

Laban's excuse had a familiar ring, echoing Rebecca's. It was better for all concerned that affairs be handled in this manner. No one could say he didn't have his daughters' interests at heart. And Jacob certainly would have enough to provide for two. Enough of what? He had asked himself that question, silently at the time, and it still perplexed him now. There had been so little untarnished love in Jacob's life, *how* could Laban have believed Jacob possessed enough of it for two?

But the thing was done, accomplished, and through the long and wasted years Jacob scrutinized its effect: Leah, with her distended frame, full of child, empty of love; Rachel, thin and panic-stricken, drawn and yet repulsed, yearning and full of infertility.

A NEW ERA

Then Joseph came. His birth cry sobbed in Jacob's heart. Suddenly, shockingly, unbelievably, a new era had begun. This child was promise, and hope, and dreams — all fulfilled and yet renewed. And in that moment out of time, Jacob tasted the Messianic ache. God, Yahweh, loomed, hovered, breathed into the face of Jacob.

He had felt this breath before and it had seared him, like fire. It had been a hot fan of flame that had scorched him, once. But he had recovered. Perhaps that had been his trouble, that he *had* recovered. Perhaps you never were supposed to.

It had happened one dark night as he was journeying to Haran, long before Rachel and Laban and Leah. Long before Joseph and all his squabbling brothers. Long before the jealousy and bitterness and anger of age. It had happened as he slept. In the intervening years he had dismissed it as but a dream. Yet, that night it had been the most real thing in his life. He had seen the Lord God Yahweh and heard him make a promise:

> "Know that I am with you; I will protect you wherever you go, and bring you back to this land. I will never leave you until I have done what I promised you" (Gen 28:15-16).

He had believed that promise, then, and had responded with a vow:

> "If God remains with me to protect me on this journey I am making and to give me enough bread to eat and clothing to wear, and I come back safe to my father's house, the Lord shall be my God" (Gen 28:20-22).

"The Lord shall be my God . . . ."

A VOW DIMINISHED

When had that vow diminished? Where had it been laid to its final resting place? What moment had enervated it of all its potent power? What event had decreed that it no longer should have life? Somewhere, amidst all the struggle, guile, and tension, fencing with Laban and Leah and his children, Jacob had decided all vows must be a sham — even the most sacred that bound you to the Lord. So he had hardened toward Yahweh his already crusty heart and had bequeathed to the realm of religion household gods and mandrake roots. And yet, he could never quite forget the dream and the promises it held — given and received. Nor could he ever quite ignore the transcendent shining out of Joseph's eyes.

That was why he now must foil Esau who was riding toward him with four hundred men. Nothing must destroy Joseph. Joseph must be saved. And so, in desperation, Jacob made his shrewd decision:

> In the course of that night, Jacob arose, took his two wives, with the two maid-servants and his eleven children and crossed the ford of the Jabbok. After he had taken them across the stream and had brought over all his possessions, Jacob was left there alone (Gen 32:23-25).

He didn't really mind. All people were alone. Some tried not to be, but it never really worked. And you were better off alone because then you were more safe. Jacob had had a lifetime practicing survival. He intended to survive tonight and then again tomorrow. He intended to bring his chosen son into his promised land.

> Then some man wrestled with him until the break of dawn. When the man saw that he could not prevail over him, he struck Jacob's hip at its socket, so that the hip socket was wrenched as they wrestled (Gen 32:25-27).

DISLOCATED AND DEFEATED

Jacob heard the snap and felt the blinding pain. He knew he had been dislocated. He knew he would never be the same. He knew he had been vanquished. Never had he fought so hard or so long to preserve something that was already gone. Never had he been so totally possessed. He had known it was coming as soon as he lay down, because he had felt the hot breath in his face, had once again known the consuming fire. He had tried to rise and run, and had been felled; had tried to inch and crawl away, and had been probed. Every rib had been numbered, every sinew counted. He had felt terror and a certain wild agony of joy; he had been severed and then been knit together, piece by piece. Every touch became a divestation and a flinching wound, as his silent adversary steadily wracked his quivering frame. He longed to cry out but had no words to speak. He tried to parry but found he had no strength. And still his conqueror wrenched, dark and luminous and terrible.

He might have died that night, had he not a stronger urge to live. And so his body never yielded, although his heart had long been won.

Then Jacob felt the snap. The trysting time was done. Dawn was here and departure and bereftness. And in a sudden tumultuous unfamiliar gesture of the heart, Jacob cried out pleadingly, clinging to his master: "I will not let you go until you bless me . . . bless me too . . . bless me too." The words echoed back through all the distant years, bringing Esau's face. And in this remembrance, Jacob humbly receives the Lord: "You shall no longer be spoken of as Jacob, but as Israel, because you have contended with divine and human beings and have prevailed." Jacob replies with awe: "I have seen God face to face, yet my life has been spared" (Gen 32:29-31)

LIMPING AWAY

"And then the man departed and Jacob limped away."

To what? To loss of Rachel in childbirth, to loss of Joseph in Egypt, to loss of future generations as slaves.

To what else? To reconciliation with his brother Esau, to reconciliation with himself and his human heart and its turbulent power to love, to reconciliation with his God.

To anything more? To witness to all modern and equally confused wrestlers with the Lord, that liberation is overpowering Love, and that our part is to yield. To proclaim that writhing struggle holds germs of ecstasy and peace. To state that limping through life, broken by the divine, can be a desirable crippling. And to aver that trysting with the Lord is always consuming engagement. To speak the words of Job, learned through his own wooing time: "I have heard of you by the hearing of the ear, but only now does my eye see you" (Job 42:5).

D. L. Lawrence once opined: "Love is the great Asker."

What did he ask of Jacob? What does he ask of you?

Esther

The brightest stars are often most alone,
    sky watchers note;
And shine most brilliantly
    when most remote.
So I, a distant dreamer
    and sky watcher, too,
Nightly search the heavens
    and spin my lore of you,
      O Esther lumines!

Around your blazing brilliance
    lesser lights rotate:
Eunuchs, vizirs, slaves,
    satellites of state;
But none can match the splendor
    of your lonely sheen:
Liberator, vindicator,
    Radiant, noble queen,
      O Esther lumines!

Ahasuerus sighted you
    was transfixed, galvanized:
Your quiet flawless gleaming;
Your lucent shimmering mind;
Your scintillating virtue,
    Enslaved him, though your Lord;
Your sphere became his orbit;
Your planet, his, adored.
      O Esther lumines!

How foolish, then, of Haman
  to try and dim your light;
  to persecute your nation;
  to usher in the night
    of death and empty vengeance —
    (jealousy's terrain)
  to plot your uncle's hanging,
    just for selfish gain.
    O Esther lumines!

Though loneliness is terrible,
  it can liberate the soul,
    can purify the heartland,
    can eek its final toll
      for a life of lustrous justice
      and integrity, so strong,
  that all one's self is given
    to right a sinful wrong.
    O Esther lumines!

And thus, you take the risk
  and plead your people's cause;
Expose ambitious lying,
  revoke its hateful laws;
Transform a day of mourning
  into one of righteous might,
And raise the hopes of Haman
  unto their hanging height.
    O Esther lumines!

And there the story ceases;
  Freedom is achieved.
Haman dies ignoble;
  Mordecai succeeds;
Ahasuerus, kingly,
  governs from his throne;
And you, refulgent beauty,
  irradiate alone.
    O Esther lumines!

The brightest stars are often loneliest,
   sky watchers note;
And shine most brilliantly
   when most remote.
So I, a lonely dreamer
   and sky watcher, too,
Nightly search the heavens
   and feel my thoughts of you,
     O Esther lumines!

A Journey Through Loneliness

Sometimes the loneliest place is to be where there are many. Sometimes the loneliest person is the most gifted and affirmed. At least, Joseph found this to be so.

Really, he should have had "everything going for him" as we are so fond of saying today. He was young, pleasing in form, quick of mind, vivid of imagination, yearning in spirit, lavishly loved by his father. He had a certain insight into personalities and events, and he wanted so much to belong to that tribe of other brothers who simultaneously revered and scorned him. Perhaps he tried too hard or perhaps he effected the wrong means. At any rate, his dreams only alienated and his scrupulous reports only enraged the very people he was trying to please—his brothers. So he became a "loner"—not by desire but by design, perhaps divine design.

THE POVERTY OF UNIQUENESS

In his slim little volume *Poverty of Spirit,* Johannes Metz speaks of the forms which such poverty can assume. Perhaps Joseph's was the "poverty of uniqueness and superiority." He had "a secret in his heart that made him great and lonely." He had "his own exceptional mission, which, because it was without parallel, offered him neither protection or guarantee among other men." He had a "call to stand alone, deprived of companionship and community."[1]

But at the age of seventeen when we first meet Joseph and hear his story, he knew none of these things. All he knew was that there existed a camaraderie of relationships which never included him, an esprit of belonging to which he was alien. And this alternately puzzled and wounded him.

His father, Jacob or Israel, tried to cloak him from this certain knowledge always present in Joseph's life—of being lonely—but seamless multi-colored robes could never quite make up for nakedness of heart. So

1. Johannes Metz, *Poverty of Spirit* (New York: Newman, 1968) 40.

even that failed. Miserably. For it was that very robe which initiated his brothers' final jealous act. "His brothers, seeing how his father loved him more than all his other sons, came to hate him so much that they could not say a civil word to him" (Gen 37:4). Nor are they able to perform a civil act.

We will never know what feelings coursed through Joseph's spirit that day of doom as he plodded over the hills to Dothan where his brothers tended the sheep. Perhaps, in the beauty of the season, he felt renewed hope. After all, he was bearing food and greetings from their father to his brothers. Perhaps as messenger of such a double blessing, he, Joseph, would somehow be accepted, if only for an afternoon. And one afternoon *could* lead to something more. So with a certain amount of optimism, he approached that rather awesome group, his community of brothers.

They, too, were watching his approach, but their aspirations for this meeting were somewhat different:

> "Here comes the man of dreams," they said to one another. "Come on, let us kill him and throw him into some well; we can say that a wild beast devoured him. Then we shall see what becomes of his dreams" (Gen 37:19-20).

SAVED BUT ENSLAVED

Thus Joseph finds himself victimized by his own. Only one of Israel's sons, Reuben, speaks against the plan, hoping, we are told, to "save him from them and to restore him to his father" (Gen 37:22-23). He is successful in that Joseph is not killed, but his ultimate desire (restoration to his father) does not come for many years. For Joseph the dreamer, the beloved of his father, the gifted imaginative spirit of Yahweh, is transported to Egypt as a slave. His felt alienation becomes literal — an Israelite among Egyptians, a slave among free men, a despised outcast among a superior race. And always, coupled with this loneliness of place is his aching loneliness of heart. *Why* had his brothers done such a deed?

It is interesting that in this pagan land, among a group of people not his own, Joseph's gifts are recognized. It is interesting that the Egyptians appreciate what his brothers could not endure. It is interesting but also rather sad. Recognition in Egypt is not the same as love in Canaan. So the loneliness prevails.

So does the injustice. His quick intelligence and organizational ability appeal to Potiphar who "put him in charge of his household, entrusting everything to him" (Gen 39:4-5). His pleasing form and manner appeal to Potiphar's wife who also wishes to entrust everything of herself to him. Joseph's words of integrity: "How could I do anything so wicked, and sin against God?" (Gen 39:9-10) serve only to place him in a second slavery — jail — as he becomes the object of the vengeful rage of a thwarted woman and her cuckolded husband.

THE TURNING POINT

So the loneliness grows: a slave in jail in an alien land, unknown, unloved, unnecessary to anyone save two other inmates, the baker and the cupbearer of Pharaoh. Some might say that this is the turning point in the Joseph story, when the downbeat is reversed. Perhaps they are right. For in correctly interpreting two different dreams, Joseph is eventually promoted and empowered by Pharaoh. But as a matter of fact, this does not occur for two years more, when it becomes advantageous for the cupbearer to "remember Joseph" and mention his name to Pharaoh. In those intervening two years, all Joseph knows is that he has been used and forgotten.

In *that* sense, however, it might very well be the turning point of the Joseph story. Because somewhere in the darkness of those two nonexistent years Joseph comes to terms with desolation, abandonment, loneliness, his destiny. He learns compassion. He sees that all men are virtually the same — weak, jealous, threatened, unfree — be they shepherds in a family of brothers, rich courtiers of Egypt with unhappy wives, or attendants to dream-tortured Pharaoh himself. The human condition is basically the same, and everyone is lonely, searching for love. In realizing this truth, Joseph is able to accept being used and discarded, available but not always wanted, affirmed for his gifts but not loved for himself. And thus he becomes ready for his mission — which is not the salvation of Egypt or Canaan. It is the salvation of his brothers.

AN EXPECTANT HEART

We all know about the fat cows and the thin ones and the seven years of plenty and famine. We all know how Joseph becomes the second most powerful man in Egypt, outranked only by Pharaoh. And we all know how prestigious that should be. But do we know how lonely it is? For Joseph is still an alien, married to an Egyptian wife of the most exclusive nobility, with sons named for his memories of the heart: Manasseh and Ephraim. In a way, he is the prototype for the New Testament prodigal father, always scanning the dusty caravans treading their way to Egypt's granary, hoping that one of them will yield a familiar face, a brother. That expectancy, that eager readiness of heart is his grace. It was the attitude with which he had approached his brothers a long time ago in the hills of Dothan. It is the attitude with which he awaits their inevitable arrival in Egypt.

They do come eventually, because all men need food, even misguided ones. In their confused hearts, they too have learned to love someone other than themselves, for they now have wives and children. Having wrenched away Joseph years ago from their father and having observed his daily pain, they too have been graced by some sort of repentant solicitude for this old man. So, for a variety of reasons they have made this arduous trip and now are before this well-dressed, well-fed, well-attended Egyptian who actually is their brother.

Joseph is not a vindictive man. Nor have his years of trial made him bitter. So why does he put his brothers through so many testings of the heart and spirit? Why does he imprison them, accuse them of spying, send for their youngest brother, frame him as a thief, and almost take him as a slave? To what purpose is all this travail?

TO COME TO COMPASSION

To help his brothers reexamine their hearts; to teach them their own personal solitude; to hollow out a place for loneliness in their lives; to cause them to experience emptiness and desolation; to aid them in knowing the pain of limitation, nonacceptance, injustice, and the broken human condition; to facilitate remembrance of their own past sins — especially the sin of betrayal of their brother and their father and themselves which they have smothered under years of selective memory; to break down their defenses so that they might cry out for forgiveness; to bring them to compassion.

It is a tortuous process, more painful for Joseph to watch and effect than it is for the brothers to experience. But once it has run its course, he hears words from his brothers' lips that obliterate years of heartache:

> "Truly we are being called to account for our brother. We saw his misery of soul when he begged our mercy, but we did not listen to him and now this misery has come home to us" (Gen 42:21-22).

Concern for themselves.

> "What can we say? How can we clear ourselves? God himself has uncovered your servants' guilt. Here we are then, my lord's slaves, we no less than the one in whose possession the cup was found" (Gen 44:16-17).

Realization of personal sin and corporate guilt.

> "Let your servant stay, then, as my lord's slave in place of the boy, I implore you, let the boy go back with his brothers" (Gen 44:33-34).

Willingness to suffer for the salvation of the life of another brother.

> "How indeed could I go back to my father and not have the boy with me? I could not bear to see the misery that would overwhelm my father" (Gen 44:34).

Compassion.

With this final declaration, this ringing verbal testimony of repentant and renewed hearts on the part of his brothers, Joseph reveals himself. His words fall gracefully from his forgiving spirit:

> "I am your brother Joseph whom you sold into Egypt. But now, do not grieve, do not reproach yourselves for having sold me here, since God sent me before you to preserve your lives" (Gen 45:5-6).

THE HEALING POWER OF LONELINESS

It is not only preservation of their physical lives about which Joseph speaks, but most importantly of their spiritual lives. Joseph, the lonely man among his brothers, has become their instrument of healing and grace.

This is not to say that Joseph will not continue to be alone, even though his brothers and father transport themselves, their families, their goods, and their livestock down to Goshen in Egypt. For Joseph's vocation seems to be intimately informed by a loneliness of the heart. Because of this, he is able to transcend the petty and non-important and to focus on the significant and eternal. And yet, there is always pain involved in such integrity: the pain of "the poverty of uniqueness." Even with his dying breath Joseph has to ask to be included. He pleads that when the Israelites leave Egypt they "be sure to take my bones from here" (Gen 50:25). He has to beg to be taken home.

Perhaps Joseph would have been less lonely had he known that his life was to become a sign. Perhaps his solitude would have been less aching had he realized initially its redemptive value. Perhaps his pain would have been less intense could he have dreamed and interpreted the end of his journey. But then, he would not have been *Joseph* and all that significant darkness of soul in which he lived so constantly would not now be a light for us. And we would never know, through him, the price and the pain and the peace that acceptance of one's solitary heart can hold for the lives of others. We would never know, through him, the healing power of loneliness. His journey would never have become ours.

Judith

I see you all compact and self-contained.
Bejeweled with the beauty of your face.
A slender form of fragile womanhood;
A mighty vessel of our Godhead's grace.
You stand before the awful dreaded foe.
You smile and he is captive to his fate.
Beguiled, seduced, disarmed by beauty's show,
He renders heart and head — decapitate!
"You are the glory of Jerusalem.
You are a noble creature of our race."
O Judith, to your praise we sing our hymn.
You witness to what goodness can displace:
When evil closes in on every side,
You urge us to your strength: in God confide.

in the Sinai

Prayer and the Desert

. . . and when they reached the wilderness of Sinai, there in the wilderness they pitched their camp; there facing the mountain Israel pitched camp (Exod 19:2).

This extremely taut position that we find Israel in — caught between the desert and the mountain — grounded in a wasteland and yet yearning for the heights — is, I think, very symbolic of the state in which we often find ourselves in prayer. And because we are not any less "stiff-necked" than our spiritual ancestors, we too often complain against God, as they did, rather than learn from our human situation the divine lesson God would teach. For the secret of the desert is that it leads to the mountain — and that we cannot circumvent it if we truly want to meet Yahweh face to face.

What does the desert teach? It teaches us (1) hunger and thirst, (2) defenselessness, (3) diminishment — none of which, in themselves, are positive states or modes of being. No one likes to go physically unsatisfied, or feel unprotected and exposed, or find oneself empty and insignificant. And yet, it is precisely by embracing these realities in our life that we are able to convert and transform them and ourselves into "theophanies" of God — which is the positive desert experience. For the desert is one of the most important ascetical "basic-training" camps we possess, if we but allow it to work its way in us — as did Moses, the great desert man of the Old Testament.

In the wilderness of arid parched terrain, both Moses and the Chosen People experience the pangs of stabbing hunger, of utter aloneness, of minuteness in the face of mighty nature. And yet, only Moses is able to elevate these purely natural phenomena to a transcendent reality. He does this by focusing on God, rather than on his tempters — who ultimately become his own people. The temptation is always the same (although varied in form) for us as well as Moses: to cry out against God and then to return to the fleshpots of Egypt, rather than patiently to await the approach to Yahweh.

For he *does* come, disguised in the very vesture we would scorn to wear. All the Israelites longed for was the human fulfillment of what they did not possess: food, protection, a country. As long as they were physically satiated, armed and victorious, on the move to the Promised Land, they were happy. Their aspirations centered on the temporal. And we are most of the time as they — satisfied with the superficial. The desert strips us of our concern for the trivial, for it removes even the essential. And then, in our vulnerability, it shifts our foundation of being, pares down our desires, and finally elevates them if, like Moses, we are sincere in our prayer-dialogue with God.

Of all the Israelites, Moses alone stands his ground with Yahweh on the shifting desert sands of popularity with the people, progress in the campaign towards Canaan, and the requirement of provident leadership. He is able to do so because, ultimately, he places no faith in these temporal aspirations. His great desert hunger and thirst is to *see Yahweh*, which is the prayerful contemplative longing of the desert pilgrim. And it is precisely his interior defenselessness mirrored in the externals of his surroundings that allows him to do this. In the "stripped down" prayer of the unfettered desert man, Moses voices the contemplative plea: "Show me your glory, I beg you" (Exod 33:18).

However, Moses does not come to this prayer easily. And unless we are willing to endure what he suffered in his journey to this Holy Ground where he meets Yahweh, we shall remain, as did the Israelites — always spectators, never participants, in the divine drama.

We must be willing, like Moses, to leave behind rank and station, friends and family, homeland and old familiar habits and trod in utter trust and expectation toward the unknown, who is God. And we must be willing to have as sentinels and signs along the way things so ephemeral as clouds, so scorching as fire, and so arid as water that is bitter. There is no map through the wilderness, except the searching human heart — and each pilgrim's footprints are obliterated by the silent shifting sands.

In the midst of a community of people like himself, Moses discovers he is alone. And that will be our experience also, as we penetrate further into the desertland of God. It is a frightening aloneness, at times, because it is so awesome and diminishing. And yet, we cannot be God's medium for others, as was Moses, unless we learn to bear his awe-filled solitude.

For the desert is the solitude of God, the bush burning yet never consumed. And the purification of the desert is immersion in that solitude and fire. And strangely it is only when we *think* that we are purgated that God truly does begin. For until that moment, it is we who have been directing the trysting in the wilderness, like Moses. And part of the purgation is to be so insecure as to strike the rock twice because we are afraid, afraid suddenly that God is as powerless as we — afraid that we will fail — that we have been deluded, that it is all a mirage. And this darkness only Yahweh's consuming fire can dispel.

Only when his human hopes have been completely obliterated, when in emptiness he learns he will never enter the Promised Land, when his people defect and worship a golden calf, when all human possibilities for success and consolation are negated, is Moses able to enter into union with Yahweh. And who of us is not afraid of such diminishment? Yet it is precisely in that moment of utter nothingness, of total loss that Moses gains *all*. In sheer poverty of soul, he raises the desert cry: "Show me your glory." And to his bold request, Yahweh responds: "I will do what you have asked, because you have won my favor and because I know you by name" (Exod 33:17).

Perhaps, in the end, that is what the desert is all about: being *known* by name to God: being fingered by him; being ravaged and ravished by him; being broken open by him; being charred by him and seared and burned and consumed. *That* is "winning his favor."

So that, when we go up the mountain, we experience only *him*. And that experience is one of all encompassing *love*.

> Yahweh passed before him and proclaimed, "Yahweh, Yahweh, a God of tenderness and compassion, slow to anger, rich in kindness and faithfulness; for thousands he maintains his kindness, forgives faults, transgression, sin . . ." (Exod 34:6-7).

Moses can only bear such an encounter with Yahweh because there is so little of Moses left — and so much of God present within him. Moses' desert vigil has, over the course of time, rendered him transparent to the Lord, which is the inevitable contemplative condition. So filled with Yahweh is he that Moses becomes the sign of God's presence among his people, even though he is initially unaware of this.

> When Moses came down from the mountain of Sinai . . . he did not know that the skin on his face was radiant after speaking with Yahweh (Exod 34:29).

So radiant is he that the people are in awe and fear to approach Moses. And so, he must wear a veil over his face so that the merely human can bear the presence of the divine.

The desert is not its own end, nor is the mountain. Both are means to a transcendent goal. Naturally speaking, both are treacherous for man. Supernaturally speaking, they are even more so. And so, we pilgrims in quest of God, must approach them with reverence and respect and not in a light or careless attitude of soul. For it is all too possible to wander aimlessly, as did the Israelites, lost in a trackless waste — or worst yet, to pitch camp, facing the mountain, but never ascending it.

For if we are sincere in our prayer, and therefore in our quest for God, we *must* ascend to meet him. It is our divine calling and destiny; not to fulfill it is to diminish ourselves forever. Paul names this encounter with the Holy One as the ultimate Christian vocation: to radiate Christ.

> And we, with our unveiled faces reflecting like mirrors the brightness of the Lord, all grow brighter and brighter as we are turned into the image that we reflect; this is the work of the Lord who is Spirit. . . . It is the same God that said: "Let there be light shining out of darkness," who has shone in our minds to radiate the light of the knowledge of God's glory, the glory on the face of Christ (2 Cor 3:18; 4:6).

We can only be "turned into the image that we reflect" if we are willing to suffer the desert experience. And always that experience is a leading by God. The desert is God's rendezvous with our soul, the place where he lures us to speak to our heart. It is there that he takes us to himself in "integrity and justice, with tenderness and love" (Hos 2:21). It is there that he teaches us his fidelity; there that we "come to know Yahweh."

And so, although it is vast and barren, we must approach it with the faith that he can make it fertile. And although it is dark and awesome, we must believe that he can light the way. And although we seem to be alone and forsaken, we must trust that he broods over us with love. For in the midst of that wilderness where we can perceive nothing but our purely human dread — awaits THE LORD — and in the distance is the mountain — where we shall see his glory — and our own.

> So hold up your limp arms and steady your trembling knees and smooth out the path you tread; . . . God himself has said: "I will not fail you or desert you," and so we can say with confidence: "With the Lord to help me, I fear nothing . . ." (Heb 12:12-13; 13:5-6).

. . . not even the desertland of God.

Ruth

Full of barley, words, and care,
  he ushered from the sheaves
  and reaped the world,
    I thought.

Harvest-god, my Boaz,
  are you the heartache's mending,
  journey's ending,
    asked for, sought?

Were winding roads,
  strange lands,
But for this threshing floor, closed door?
  Then knead me.

Plant your sandal
  on my ground.
For Naomi's sake
(mine now) receive me.

And then the deed
  was drawn.
He and I belonged
  to David's ages.

The Jonathan Time: On Reconciliation

I remember the day I first saw David — a day not unlike this one. Father and I were preparing, as usual, for war. In retrospect it seems that I have spent most of my young years warring: fighting the Philistines, fighting Goliath, fighting the jealous rages which consumed my father's heart. I have always thought that fact to be ironic — that I who so deeply hated turmoil should find myself so frequently in the midst of it. But then my whole life turns on irony, as does my death today.

There probably will be much written about these tumultuous events — these cataclysmic wars that tore a nation apart — but today, in these last lucid moments of remembering, I prefer to recount the story of an enigmatic love.

And so I turn to David, recalling that first brilliant moment when he stepped into the field, defenseless and unafraid. I have seen since then so many times that look upon his face, that powerful defenselessness that made a giant quake. He slew Goliath that day with a single slingshot stone, but the echo of that pebble was mightier than an army's roar:

Saul has killed his thousands;
And David his tens of thousands.

In that victorious instant none of us could have known, could possibly have foreseen that in ridding us of one monster, David brought to birth another: the hydra-headed jealousy latent in my father's heart.

That was the tragedy of it all: my father *did* love David, loved him as his son, his brother, his friend, his other self; he loved in David all that he, Saul, *was*, and all that he, Saul, never could become. There is a danger in that kind of love, and we acknowledge it here today. After years of strife and pain, we now say there was excess. But, as always, it is too late for remedy. My father is dead; David is gone; I have failed; and the enemy has won.

THE ENEMY WITHIN

When I say "enemy" I do not mean those perennial Philistines whom we seem never to subdue, who always plague and haunt us. No, they are tangible foes whom one can put a sword to or through, whom one can see and touch. I speak, rather, of the enemy contained inside one's heart — the capacity for darkness we all bear within, the evil of the divided and unknown self. And who can conquer that?

I tried. I would not want you to think that I became detached, a spectator at the drama of hearts rent asunder. No, I played my part — heroically, some chroniclers may later say — but however well or poorly I carried out my role, I tried with all my natural talents to execute my part.

What was that part, you ask? What role did I assume? Did I have the major lead? Was I the hero or the villain?

Ironically again, there were no gruesome villains present — only good men groping blindly for the truth. And in that search I tried to be the one who brought the healing, the reconciling agent between my father and my friend.

You see, I loved David, too — loved him as I never had or ever would love anyone again. He had that ability, you know, to engender love. And I loved my father also — that once magnificent king who slowly and agonizingly divested himself of power. And so I used to ask myself achingly in the solitude of my heart: "Why does there have to be so much pain involved in simple loving?"

In the beginning, I think that I was somewhat arrogant, for I believed that eventually *I* could breach the gap. I guess that is always the fault of untried youth — the belief that in the end *my way* must prevail. My way was reconciliation; talking things out; facing fears honestly; admitting brokenness; allowing healing. My way was saying that my father's day was over; repenting for past sins; accepting Samuel's words; yielding to Yahweh and his will. My way was peace for all: for the nation, for the army, for the citizens, for the heart. My way was saying *Amen* to the past and *Yes* to the future. And in the present my way was to love enough to heal the hurt.

MUCH TO LEARN

But I had much to learn. I had to learn that there are some chasms in a life no one can throw a bridge over; some depths too deep for sounding; some gloom no light can penetrate. I had to learn that some men continually seek success and adulation, and rage incoherently when it is bestowed on others. I had to learn that some human beings live most of their lives inhumanly, carrying about fragmented hearts beneath majestic fronts. And I had to learn that even those anointed by Yahweh and his prophets, by their family and their friends, by their nation and its people can bear within their spirits the destructive force of evil. I had to learn that sometimes in the last analysis even love is insufficient to do away with sin.

It was my father who taught me all of this. Yet I have only memories of loving him. He loved me, too, in his own distorted fashion, and if that is all a man is capable of, should we not accept it? He even used that love for me as a weapon aimed at David, angered that I took so little care for my inheritance. He berated me once, furiously, that David would usurp my throne. He did not realize that already I had given it as a gift.

For you see, between David and me there existed so much honesty, so much pure integrity, so much understanding love. He knew just as I did that he would certainly rule, succeed my father in my place and unite the kingdom. I never could have done so; kingship was not my gift; but I would have served him loyally had I been given the opportunity.

Perhaps, someday, men will say I *did* serve loyally and gave my life in fulfillment of that service. But I am dying here today close to my now dead father, far away from David, who does not even know. So you will understand how dark my insight is when all around me and within me lie the ravages of hatred.

MY INTERCESSIONS

How many times I attempted to forestall this moment. How many times I tried to prevent the now inevitable conclusion. Once, after warning David, who fled for his life, I stepped between him and my father's rage, to intercede for both. Father never realized this: that in pleading for David I was really pleading for him. He could never see what always loomed large before my eyes — that David *would* prevail, and that the only question was: Would Saul yield to him with grace? So that was the object of all my intercessions; that was the goal that brought courage to my spirit. I did not want my father to die as he did today — crying for his armor-bearer to end his blinding pain. I wanted to spare him the tragic hero's fate of always perceiving too late his consuming tragic flaw. But all my reconciling efforts were always too short-lived, always bound by time, always contingent on my father's moods and rages. And because he never was able to heal himself of these, I could never heal him either of their dark effects. And so, writhing within himself, my father lashed out at the person dearest to his heart — David. (For I always knew him to be more son to Saul than I.)

I, who was only in the end companion and friend to both, loved both of them greatly and suffered equally their pain.

Inevitably, it was always David who best bandaged the wounds, who best spoke the words which could assuage my father's heart. Always it was David, broken in spirit by estrangement, who could cry out to the estranged spirit within my father's breast. Perhaps I should have learned the lesson inherent in those moments — that ultimately only broken people can heal each other's pain. But I was broken, too—broken in my failed attempts to bring two such friends together; broken in my failed attempts to bring two such hearts to union; broken in my failed attempts to be both loyal son and brother.

So finally David went away for good until Yahweh should vindicate his cause. And when the Philistine cohorts attacked, I donned my father's armor.

Had David been fighting with and for us today, we never should have lost. My father would be commanding still vast numbers of our army. And I should not be remembering now the past, under darkening skies. But David is not here. Somewhere, far away in safety, he awaits this dreadful news, although he does not even know he waits. Nor does he know of my last thoughts, how much they center on him, and of how bereft I already feel at being unable to say farewell.

I said earlier that our beginning time and our ending time is similar— "a day not unlike this one." But the pain and the tears that have stretched between have made the years taut with expectancy. I had hoped for a different conclusion although I expected the one that is. I had longed for a different denouement although I accepted the one that must be.

And yet there is still a part of me that cries out against wasted love and an equally deep part of me that refuses to accede to defeat. So you will excuse me if I choose to believe that my death holds meaning and purpose. And you will accept the loyalty of heart which embraces Saul in his vision.

You ask: "Will the healer ever know if reconciliation has come?" And I reply: "It is not his to know, only to work to that end."

You protest that the end is unfair, that I the healer should live. And I reply that healing takes pains, sometimes the death-pains of love.

You inquire politely: "Do I not rebel at having so short a life?" And I respond that I had days enough—all of the Jonathan time.

* * *

And David lifted up his voice and wept:

> "Saul and Jonathan, beloved and cherished,
>   separated neither in life nor in death . . . .
> "I grieve for you, Jonathan my brother!
>   most dear have you been to me . . . ."
> "Saul and Jonathan, beloved and cherished,
>   separated neither in life nor in death . . . ." (2 Sam 1:23, 26).

Susanna

O shimmering swan of beauty
    abluting in the pond,
    arching your whiteness
        to the sky,

(O Susanna,
 Don't you cry to me;
 For we are bound to lying
 Under the mastic tree.)

Lovely line of limb
   and flawless form,
   sinuously, sinlessly,
      you lie.

(O Susanna,
 Don't you cry to me;
 For we are bound to lying
 Under the holm oak tree.)

O emblematic woman,
   female sign,
   of innocence unveiled,
   design transgressed;

(O Susanna,
 Don't you cry to me.)

You lift your eyes to heaven,
   heave a sigh,
   for all the wrongs toward women,
   unredressed.

(For we will have you dying
  Under the mastic tree.)

O paragon most pure,
  consummate lust
  has driveled at your shrine,
  besmirched your name;

(O Susanna,
  Don't you cry to me.)

You stand defenseless,
  naked, unadorned,
  the public image
  of a private shame.

(For we will have you dying
  Under the holm oak tree.)

How many women
  stripped, desired, consumed,
  have struggled with the evil
  you have known!

(O Susanna,
  Don't you cry to me.)

How many women
  raped in heart and soul
  have screamed for Daniel,
  yet found they were alone.

(For we will have you dying
  Under the Eros Tree.)

Your vindication, wife inviolate,
  betrays corruption to its counterpart:
  the leering eye, the salivating mind,
  the lusting license in a lecherous heart.

(O Susanna,
  Won't you cry for me?)

Your praise resounds, O beauty unseduced,
   beyond the corners of your garden glade;
   like ripples from your unpolluted pond,
   the song you craft,
   sings, swells, and never fades.

(For I am doomed to die
Under the Evil Tree.)

Its lilting notes reverberate, then fall,
   then rise again
   intoned by every youth,
   who harmonizes puberty, desire,
   in the counterpunctal chords
      of grace and truth.

(O Susanna,
Won't you pray for me?
And sing your Song of Goodness
Under the Judgment Tree.)

Davidic Diminishment: Something to Do with Love

Always it had something to do with love — and the reaching for it, he thought. Even this girl lying beside him, Abishag, slight and afraid, bespoke love's last tribute: "Let some young girl be found for the king . . . she shall lie on your breast and keep the king warm." As if anything could warm his brittle bones now — or his flaccid spirit. He smiled ruefully. There had been a time past, not so long ago, when such a beauty would have stirred everything in him — heart, sinews, glands. But that was yesterday and this today: Abishag beside him like blue-veined marble, cold and beautiful, petrified and appalled at his dying.

At his dying. The words seized him. How long he had reached for that — his mentor — death. Restlessly he plucked the coverlet and their images rose before him: Saul and Jonathan; Goliath and Uriah; his infant son and his grown one, Absalom — all dead and gone — all hauntingly alive.

He dozed and mused. Perhaps any stretching out for love was a stretching out for death — two sides of life's one gold coin. Well, he had spent it all — his life — lavishly, painfully, totally, with no compromise. He had taken everything: pain, loneliness, sin; beauty, music, love; war, kingship, fatherhood; the desert, the mountains, the caves. He had danced and plundered and prayed and lusted and loved and laughed and sung. And he had wept and lamented, too — the price of living. But increasingly, he had done so with a solitary heart.

He had always sensed an irony in this — a king surrounded day and night by warriors, servants, guards, and wives — yet always so totally alone. Alone in what he felt and what he did — unique in the complexity of a heart and mind and soul that fragmented into separation. Well, he had never boasted that he was one, nor had he ever claimed perfection. Even now, at the end, he was unable to effectively discern what single mode of life, simply lived, would have made him whole: the shepherd's? the warrior's? the king's? the mystic's? the musician's? the family man engendering his sons? Which one held the answer, the surcease to his searching?

in the Sinai

The fire fanned upward and warmth drowsed over him. A cup held to his lips; hot wine running rivulets down his throat. In the corner, a slave boy playing music. And David was with his sheep.

* * *

Banked against the hills with his bread and cheese beside him, he was intent upon his reed. It had become his friend, a fellow solitary, silent, or conversant, dependent on its master's mood. They shared a brotherhood together, David and his reed, more real and lively than any that might exist at home. Seven older brothers jostling for recognition made David ill at ease. So it was with secret gratitude mingled with relief that he had embraced the shepherd's life: hills and sky and sheep and silence. The music of his reed and the music of his thoughts and the music of his clouds. It all belonged to him as much as did the cold and damp and certain loneliness. He had grown hardy here; had developed toughened muscles and strengthened sinews; had learned to weather and endure without self-pity or neglect; had learned to forecast, fortify, and protect; had learned how one prevails.

But today his reed complained, sang false and flat — and so he was distracted. Bent over, totally absorbed, with his slingshot thrown carelessly aside, he failed to sense the danger. A horrible bleating filled the air, rent the silence, pierced his heart. Wide-eyed, disbelieving, he fumbled for his weapon but to no avail. The kill had been complete and there before him, jawed and plundered, already borne away, he saw his mangled sheep. Fury stung him; rage engulfed him; and with hot tears streaming down his cheeks, he pursued the powerful beast.

After the event he often wondered what mythic strength possessed him. Had it indeed been David, the youthful shepherd boy who had tracked and felled the lion, forced open its death-clamped jaws, and removed his pitiful sheep? They had found him thus at evening (missing flock and boy) keeping anguished vigil, weeping and bereaved.

For a long time after, he was inconsolable, although his family did not notice. Respectfully he listened as his father Jesse spoke and nodded at the wisdom of one sheep against a flock, though he never quite believed it. That one sheep had life and that life had been entrusted to his care, and he had failed that care and so that life had failed. For many days after that his reed played melancholy and his sky had subtle shadows and his flock was incomplete. Death had reared its ugly head and had leered at David's soul.

* * *

That had been before — before the aftermath — before the strange beginning of a life no more his own. The day they had come running for him had been a cloudless one, brilliant blue and shimmering, nature's gift to man. He had forgotten food that morning, so eager was his spirit to anticipate the dawn. And so the servant waving to him from the second distant hill had meant no more than surcease from his hunger pangs; thoughtful Jesse sending bread and perhaps some fresh made cheese. He waved a quick response as the servant crowned the nearest hill, and now the wind breathed words: "Your father Jesse wants you home." And thus he left his sheep and his brief idyllic life and came to Samuel's horn and Yahweh's fiery oil.

That moment was his marriage and his wedding night combined. Yahweh embraced him and David was consumed. "The spirit of Yahweh seized on David and stayed with him from that day on."

And therein lay the ache of it and the tantalizing torment: Yahweh playing on David's soul, one musician to another. "I am his instrument," the boy would think, "my life is not my own."

But they were only words and words often miss the mark. It was reality that counted and the daily grit and grind, where clarity was dubious and motives self-deceptive. So he never quite was sure why he climbed the hills that day and strained to catch a glimpse of the dreaded Philistine.

* * *

Perhaps incipient manhood drove him to the fray. (One can stay the youngest only for so long.) Or did a deeper challenge than even Goliath could command summon him to dare to flaunt the giant's wrath? He never knew the reason except that he was driven — driven to contend with forces greater than his own. Nor did he realize then as he selected his smooth stones that he was picking out a pattern that would govern all his days: reaching out to love in some relentless fashion, even as he once had grimly tracked his sheep.

And so he contemplated stones as he had reflected on his reed — with absolute absorption — given to the deed. Only wariness was here, now, and vulnerability a shield. And when he met Goliath, deadliness was formed. "Then David triumphed over the Philistine with sling and stone and struck the Philistine down and killed him."

He used to see it in his dreams until they wakened him to nightmare: the head rolling in the dust; his bloody hand with sword. And in the gentle dark he would feel his trembling limbs and smell his clammy sweat and know he was alive. The familiar accouterments of a soldier's life clamped themselves about him — images and visions of Death stalking out a field. And in the night he'd ask what daylight could never bring to question: what or whom had compelled him to choose this sort of life?

Was it Samuel, Yahweh, the oil — or something more than these? And then a burnt log smoked and hissed the name of Saul.

* * *

Saul, splendid and mighty, ravenous and broken, but still, in the beginning, god-like and sublime. He had looked up that dreadful day (which he had made victorious) proffering Goliath's head, into the face of Saul. And life suddenly took on meaning. Beyond sheep and reeds and brothers — beyond anointing, Samuel, Yahweh — there was a human meaning and it framed the face of Saul. And David loved him simply, totally, and forever. Goliath dead; Saul alive. Simultaneously, once again, death and love had met, inextricably entwined. He never knew till later that love's teeth are like the lion's. By then his heart was mangled. Internal bleeding had begun.

But for a time it was so very beautiful. They rode together to battles like a father and his son, and in the evening in Saul's tent, David would play upon his harp. And Jonathan and he, brothers in blood, had pledged their solemn word and sealed it with an oath. And so, for just a little while, David's heart would leap for joy. And then, gradually, the nightmares lessened because the day ones had begun.

* * *

The old king muttered feverishly and twisted on his bed. Some sort of broken song echoed from out some broken past: "Saul has killed his thousands, and David his tens of thousands."

However, it never really started there. It had existed long before in Saul: the insecurity, the pain of melancholy, the rejection by Yahweh, the feeling of being finished and disposed of. It was plainly obvious that Jonathan was no leader nor did he want to be. David as the people's choice was logical. Years later David knew all this and understood the cause. But never was he able to accept it nor to cease the pain and loving. And as the drama played itself he came to face the truth — that in the combat of this terrible foe, the beast of love gone sour, David first knew evil. It filtered through the atmosphere, this subtle jealous poison. It garbed the form of Saul and cloaked his thoughts and deeds. It stagnated words and formed cesspools of desire. It gushed like angry torrents and eroded rock-like friendships. It seeped into the mind's crevices and spawned a brood of maggots. And it slowly killed the best in them — Jonathan, Saul, and David.

Probably, at the deepest core, there is resentment in all love, most certainly in love which is profound. There is a terrible risk in radicalizing anything — above all things — the heart. But at the moment when Saul's life and his met and intersected, David was unaware. He only knew how much he cared and how much he would surrender of his heart to love this man. And so he did — irrevocably — and became love's lonely victim. Always it had something to do with love — and the reaching for it.

But the question coiled serpentine for the remainder of his life: Whatever had possessed Saul to choose him once and then reject him as his friend? Round and round through the years, this cry crisscrossed his heart. And forever, till his dying day, David would remember: the pain; the anguished supplications; the spear hurtling through the air toward him; the malicious face of Saul; the hiding out; Jonathan as go-between; the awful loneliness and terror; the spying and the treachery; sparing Saul for love, twice; the tears of reconciliation; the homecoming — and then — the pattern viciously renewed. Until the final day: David gone, the Philistine attack, Saul and Jonathan dead — mangled sheep. And David weeping, weeping, weeping — for the past and for the future — changed and never again heart-whole, lost and forever lonely. The tragedy of what never should have been. The lion and the sheep once more — and David — lost and broken. Death and love entwined.

They found him thus when they came to name him as their king. And he went with them because . . . there was nothing else to do.

***

It was very easy, then, to give yourself to war. Carving out a kingdom was simpler than healing up a heart. And so he started conquering — David the war lord, the man who had once been the gentle shepherd boy.

Always it had something to do with love and the reaching for it. For a long time after nothing could console him but the vastness of the desert and the psalms welling from his heart. And so he sang as he encamped for a night underneath the stars:

"Yahweh, what is man that you should notice him?
A human being that you should think about him?
Man's life, a mere puff of wind,
His days, as fugitive as shadows."

Puffs of wind and shadows from a heart hiding out.

***

And then one ecstatic day the harp sang a happy song plucked straight from David's heart, and he reached for her and held her close. Her name was Bathsheba.

He should have known there was evil now pulsating through his veins. Blood-letting does this quietly. All life becomes a battlefield. You cling to what you hold although she is another's wife.

His thoughts were tangled now as they had been before. The night was torrid, but she had bathed and her coolness flooded him. Yes, she loved Uriah but David wore the crown, and she was such a jewel — precious, rare, well formed and multi-faceted. Light and beauty gleamed from her.

Repose surrounded her. She never questioned or denied; she only came to yield. And when he crushed her to him, she cut across his heart and splintered it. So he looked sin in the face and found her soft and warm. Always it had something to do with love — and the reaching for it.

He had never meant for death to haunt their bed. He had had enough of carnage and battles of the heart. Nor was he even sure he meant to marry her. But the child was his, and Uriah was too upright and intuitive to break Mosaic law no matter how cleverly enticed. So David gave the order and then the deed was done. "Bathsheba mourned Uriah's death. And when the mourning period was over, David sent for her and brought her into his house. And she became his wife and bore him a son." So now there were two more sheep led to slaughter, Uriah and the child. Nathan's apt parable opened all the wounds: a sheep and shepherd theme. And when David knelt and wept, they all were lying there: his little lamb; Saul and Jonathan; Uriah and David's baby son; Bathsheba and her pain. And David knew he had become a lion and Philistine — rapacious and destructive — love and death entwined. "On the seventh day, the child died."

***

Repentance is a long and lonely road. He trod it daily. Even little Solomon, their second darling son, recalled to him their first, the child never known, never grown because of David's sin. So he walked a narrow line, finely drawn within, that he himself had marked, between love and its expression. He was more frequently away now, more frequently withdrawn, and while tender with Bathsheba, he had no more desire. Instead, anxiously, he watched his other brood of boys born from other wives and sensed their rivalry, their jealousy, their vying for attention. And he remembered Yahweh's words and knew them to be true: "The sword shall never depart from your house." David's punishment bequeathed unto his sons.

***

And then the horror broke: Amnon and Tamar; Amnon and Absalom; Absalom and David: incest, fratricide; son against his father. Love and death entwined.

He should have censured Amnon, but being his first-born and favored, he let him go unchecked: the fond father's folly. He should have talked with Absalom and cautioned him with reason, but instead he ignored his rage: the fearful father's folly. Knowing firsthand, the ravages of sin; knowing so well the terrible twistedness that beauty, love, and lust contort, he found himself ashamed and turned away. And so the violence spawned: Amnon murdered; Absalom in flight. David, life weary, saw the end in sight.

* * *

Dusk filled the room. Another log thrown upon the fire. Outside the wind sighs; a tree branch shakes, shudders, startling the king.

* * *

The final hour of doom: Absalom hanging by a branch, three pikes thrust through his heart, and David weeping, weeping, inconsolable: "My son Absalom: Absalom, my son! If only I had died instead of you, Absalom, my son!" The tragedy of what never should have been: Absalom like Saul, wanting to be king; Absalom like David, seizing what was not his; Absalom like Amnon and all the other sheep — mangled and dead before their time. Love and death entwined.

* * *

The room whirled before his eyes, then straightened. Two pillars detached themselves, moved forward, then stopped. Nathan and Bathsheba, whispering.

Weariness flooded him — weariness with life, with all the machinations, politics, treacheries, and ambitions of a family and a nation. Internal and external strife — at the beginning and the end. Was there nothing more to living — to his living? No other legacy? Well, then let it be Solomon if that is what they want — for Bathsheba's sake and Nathan's and for the inexplicable design. Choose him; call him; crown him; least of all his brothers in claim and in renown — like his father once had been. His blood is mine; his mistakes will be his own. Let it be.

* * *

And then the room grew crowded and filled with shuffling murmur. There was a velvet darkness draped around the night, and before a vivid bonfire David saw a ray of light weaving in a dance, sinuously. Huge throngs clapped and played and plucked their lyres and harps. The tambourines grew feverish; the dancer writhed and twisted. With agonized limbs, he stretched and then contorted. Pain rippled up his arms and flooded over his face, tortuously. The man would break! The music reached a fever; the dancer spun and whirled, then slowly wound to ending. A pause. The music stopped. Life breathed in together, rested.

And then, from far away a little reed began to sing, way beyond the hills. Its sweetness soothed. The dancer wiped his brow and the terror left his eyes. He poised and turned eagerly, as if waiting for a friend. The music grew in waves of beauty, radiantly. Joy was there and the first fresh dew of life. And love was there beyond the hurt and pain. And awe was there for Someone mighty enough to govern stars and yet know the heart of man.

And relief was there for hearing that we do not go alone through ache and disillusion. And then the reed played low, but very clear and gentle, of how much Yahweh can forgive in hearts that break and weep.

The dancer's head was bowed and tears flowed down his face. And there was stillness.

And then the reed gathered to the fullness of a sea and surged up the flames and the throng and all the night. The fire burned upward like a huge and noble pillar and high above it gleaming was the Ark, a glittering star.

And David raised his head and gazed into the fire and saw them all again: his little bleating sheep and then, the noble lion; Jesse and his brothers; Goliath, head intact; Uriah with a baby boy; Absalom alive and hugging Amnon. And then the fire roared and broke: a little space between two mighty brilliant flames. And David saw them both, Saul and Jonathan, father and brother, holding out their hands. They called to him with joy and opened wide their arms, and over them like a golden shaft shimmered Yahweh's Ark. The music rose and swelled, lifted to a peak. And David stretched and reached and yearned out to the Light. And then, ecstatically, the reed broke its golden sound, and with a mighty surge of love, David leaped into the fire.

And then joy broke his heart and the reed gave up its song. "Love is victorious. Love conquers all. Amen."

near Church of the Holy Sepulcher
Jerusalem

The Widow

She dwells in Zarephath,
　　Naim, Jerusalem —
　　or any place of need.
She is the widow
　　of nobility, majestic mite,
　　in what she can forsake,
　　expend, give back, or lend.

Elijah gained from her
　　some food, a room,
　　the boon of company,
　　security and rest.
He repaid her with his best:
　　her son reborn.

Jesus, first surprised,
　　then moved,
　　watched two such women
　　lose the leaven of their years —
　　all that they held dear:
　　son; income.

Each he blessed
　　in unguessed power:
One's son restored to life;
　　the other raised to heights
　　of praise:
Gospeled for our age.

From nothing, all.
　　Beyond recall.

Ah! To be bereft
　　and left
　　with only God.

"Pneumatic Fascination": The Elijah within Us

In a provocative essay on "The Person of the Holy Spirit,"[1] Heribert Mühlen, a German theologian, speaks of the interaction of "pneumatic fascination" and an encounter with the Lord. Although he strictly defines pneumatic fascination in relation to the Jesus experience, it is possible to trace the outlines of this movement through an Old Testament prophet of the Lord: Elijah.

Mühlen delineates the rhythm of pneumatic fascination as alternating between a fear/joy tempo. Simultaneously, one experiences both attraction and withdrawal in connection with the fascinating object or person. Such a feeling, Mühlen states, is fundamental to all human existence, and he concludes that "for the most part we become truly involved only when something or someone *continually* fascinates us."[2]

Viewed in a religious light, Jesus Christ will be always the most pneumatically fascinating of men. But centuries before his arrival, looming large in shadowy form, Elijah, prophet of the Lord, expressed this pneumatic fascination for others and experienced it within himself. Such an inspired tension, manifested and integrated within the community, has much to say to us as potential prophets of our twentieth century. For Elijah's history could be ours.

ELIJAH'S GROWTH

Significantly, an initial encounter with the prophet in the first book of Kings depicts him as a somewhat brash and over-confident individual. Certainly he has received the spirit of Yahweh, for his opening conversation deals with a predicted drought which, in fact, does occur. And certainly, as Yahweh's instrument, he must possess a certain degree of openness and

---

1. Heribert Mühlen, "The Person of the Holy Spirit," *The Holy Spirit and Power: The Catholic Charismatic Renewal*, ed. Kilian McDonnell, O.S.B. (New York: Doubleday & Company, Inc., 1975) 11–33.
2. *Ibid.*, 22.

receptivity to the Lord. Yet there is about Elijah an element of "self-control," almost an attitude of self-conceit, that highlights a lack of humility at the charism he has received. To that extent the Elijah story is not so much a rendition of what Elijah does to and for the community as God's emissary, but rather a revelation of what God does to and for Elijah to render him more deeply his "breath." As such, it is a narrative of growth: Elijah's growth into his charism.

Weaving its way throughout the tale is the thread of an ironic twist, and it is just this "reversal motif" that serves to keep Elijah unsettled and periodically ill at ease. This very state of unbalance, of always jockeying for dominant control in the Elijah-God relationship, constitutes, early on, the pneumatic fascination integral to Elijah's dealings with the Lord.

For the most part, Elijah enjoys serving as the mouthpiece of Yahweh. It is only occasionally that he fears with an awful dread the consequences of such a vocation. One such occasion revolves around the Wadi Cherith sojourn.

A DROUGHT

Elijah has adamantly predicted a drought and, indeed, his words have been vindicated. No rain falls on the land. Elijah, however, is safe. At the injunction of Yahweh he has hidden himself near a flowing stream. Ravens bring him "bread in the morning and meat in the evening, and he quenched his thirst at the stream" (1 Kgs 17:6). The scene could hardly be more idyllic to the reader nor more satisfying to the prophet. The drought *did* come; he *was* right; *all* is under control — *Elijah's control*. It is at just such a complacent moment that Yahweh intrudes: "the stream dried up" — and suddenly we are given the picture of a frustrated man whose "fascination" with the Lord has overwhelmingly turned to fear. Elijah is immensely puzzled. How can he assail the Unassailable? How can he fathom the Inscrutable? Unsettled, and with a certain amount of awe, Elijah again becomes subservient to the inspiration of Yahweh. He *waits*, waits for Yahweh's dictates, dependent and in need.

Yahweh's word finally comes to the God-thirsting prophet and Elijah is ordered to go to Zarephath and there befriend a widow. Elijah is glad to befriend anyone at this moment, especially someone who will harbor him, and so, with alacrity, he sets off for Sidon. There he finds all as Yahweh had promised and so he prophesies to his downcast landlady:

"Jar of meal shall not be spent,
jug of oil shall not be emptied,
before the day when Yahweh sends
rain on the face of the earth" (1 Kgs 17:14).

Elijah's good fortune and trust in the Lord are transmitted jubilantly through him to the widow. For a while, all is again well. Elijah settles in, happy to be provided for and once again vindicated. There is food; there is shelter; there is honor; there is companionship. And the jar of meal does not run out — just as Elijah had said.

A DEATH

This time, with Yahweh's intrusion, the irony is darker, the joke grimmer, the reversal more startling. Elijah is not merely taken off balance; he is literally stunned. The widow's son dies, and the distraught woman berates Elijah, blaming him for the death. "What quarrel have you with me, man of God? Have you come here to bring my sins home to me and to kill my son?" (1 Kgs 17:18-19) Appalled, Elijah in turn berates God: "Yahweh, my God, do you mean to bring grief to the widow who is looking after me by killing her son?" (1 Kgs 17:20-21) Elijah is overwhelmed. Without warning, that provident, beneficent God who so fascinates and tantalizes the prophet has become an object of terror. Yahweh has inexplicably withdrawn his favor and the abyss of that horror compels Elijah to posit the unutterable question: Why?

Yahweh makes no response, which *is* his response. In the immensity of that eloquent silence, Elijah is again humbled. He assumes the receptive stance: he begs. "Yahweh my God, may the soul of this child, I beg you, come into him again" (1 Kgs 17:21-22). With the utterance of this humble plea, the instrument becomes so. Yahweh, through Elijah, returns life to the child. Through this act on the part of Yahweh the balance is once more restored — or so Elijah thinks. Fear subsides; joy returns; Yahweh's spirit is calmed.

And "a long time went by . . ." (1 Kgs 18:1).

Suddenly, again without warning, the Timeless intersects with time. Elijah is called once more to witness, but on a far larger scale. "The word of Yahweh came to Elijah . . . 'Go, present yourself to Ahab'" (1 Kgs 18:1). And thus begins Elijah's most prophetic experience to date: the sacrifice on Mount Carmel and the consequent storm of rain. But fast on the thrill of the blazing fire and the destruction of the prophets of Baal comes the edict of the vengeful Jezebel: Elijah is to be killed.

CREATUREHOOD

It is this final twist of the always reversible thread, this downbeat of the ever recurring fascination theme, this hot breath of Yahweh scorching him asunder that causes Elijah to finally lose heart. All his human resources are played out; Elijah realizes *creaturehood.* "He was afraid and he fled for his life" — the ineluctable nadir experience of a person. In near despair at the desolation of his apparent abandonment by God, Elijah calls out from under the furze bush: "Yahweh, I have had enough. Take my life; I am no better than my ancestors" (1 Kgs 19:4-5). Paradoxically, it is this moment that Yahweh has been awaiting in the life of Elijah, the moment of total surrender: "take my life"; the moment of humble self-perception: "I am no better than my ancestors"; the moment of completed fascination: "I have had enough." Elijah concedes: Yahweh has won.

Out of the exhaustion of such profound wrestling with his God and through the upheaval of such concomitant loss and victory, Elijah falls into a deep sleep. He is awakened to learn, ironically enough, that it is out of the culminating effect of all of these diverse experiences—the Wadi, the widow, the fire and the rain—that Elijah has been readied for the ultimate encounter with Yahweh on Mount Horeb. All of these previous interludes with the Lord were, Elijah discovers, but tantalizing preludes to the one, great, fascinating, dreaded, and joy-filled rendezvous with his God.

THE GENTLE BREEZE

The final joke, the ultimate twist, after three successive experiences with the power and might of Yahweh, is that Elijah, in wonder-filled amazement perceives that the Lord is also in the "gentle breeze" (1 Kgs 19:13).

It is in this moment of tender realization that Elijah is divinely commissioned as instrument for the nation: "You are to go and anoint Hazael as king of Aram. You are to anoint Jehu son of Nimshi as king of Israel, and to anoint Elisha son of Shaphat, of Abel Meholah, as prophet to succeed you" (1 Kgs 19:16-17). No longer is Elijah to be self-concerned with petty interests and trivial desires: food, shelter, acceptance. He has been taken from out of himself and transformed for the service of others. From the Wadi to Horeb has been a long journey and at times a wearying one. But unknown to Elijah, at each step of the way he has been traversing the country of God. And thus, paradoxically, but rightly enough, he has come to the heartland of people.

In our own experiential pneumatic fascination with the person of Jesus Christ, there is much we can learn from the colorful story of one of his Father's prophets. For there is an Elijah buried deep within us, who is alternately tantalized and repelled by the Lord; who periodically speaks with God's breath and God's Spirit and then, mistakenly, calls it his own; who has to learn through repeated "singeings" that a prophet lives, not for himself, but for others.

The story of Elijah holds rich promise for us, charismatic prophets of the new dispensation. For if we too but yield to fascination of God, his power will transform us, scorching though his fire might be.

> We possess the prophetic message as something altogether reliable. Keep your attention closely fixed on it, as you would on a lamp shining in a dark place until the first streaks of dawn appear and the morning star rises in your hearts (2 Pet 1:19).

Hannah

An empty womb was only half the pain;
It was the empty heart that ached most deep.
And bearing scorn from other pregnant maids

Whose bellies swelled with seed mine couldn't keep.
So if I yearly trod the Temple ground,
And if I cried and often would not eat,

It was because my life could hear no sound
Of childish laughter; little circling arms
Would never reach for me nor wrap me round.

Nor was I fertile through the mandrake charms.
So I implored my God and made a vow
(With many tears that Eli was alarmed!)

"Give me a child, a man-child me allow;
I consecrate him to your service, Lord.
He will be yours; my promise I avow."

If only you might hear my pleading word."
And Yahweh opened up my womb with joy
And acted on his servant with accord:

He blessed me with my prophet-baby-boy!
And now I sing a song which never ends:
"The humble poor God's favor will enjoy.

The proud and haughty never he befriends.
I praise him for his mercy and his love!
With peace and joy from pain, he makes amends.

O raise my song to Yahweh God above!
The barren woman feels his fruitful touch;
I praise him for his mercy and his love."

Running with Jonah: A Drama in Three Acts

Had Jonah lived in our century, he doubtless would have been a devotee of "running for health and fitness." For although he is the antagonist of the shortest narrative in Scripture, he covers as much geographical, psychological, and spiritual distance as any of his fellow prophets or harbingers of Yahweh.

Perhaps it is because his story is so bluntly and humorously told that we find ourselves identifying with this belligerent little man who abhors being *called*. Perhaps, also, we discover that there is a part of Jonah in each of us. At any rate, he is hard to resist liking, in spite of all his petulance.

Obviously, his is an impulsive personality. "The word of Yahweh was addressed to Jonah . . . . 'Up!' he said, 'Go to Nineveh, the great city, and inform them that their wickedness has become known to me.'" Jonah has no hesitation whatsoever when he discerns Yahweh's call. Immediately, he goes — as far away from Nineveh as he can get. "Jonah decided to run away from Yahweh, and to go to Tarshish," which (as we are told) represented for the Hebrews the end limits of the world. So off he runs down to the harbor, pays his fare, and boards the ship. He has shaken from his feet forever the shackles of prophethood. Now he is a free man.

And so the voyage begins, along with the great drama of "Jonah vs. Yahweh," which is played out in minute detail before a varied array of spectators. Jonah, however, is complacent. He has made his decision and now is at peace.

"But Yahweh unleashed a violent wind on the sea, and there was such a great storm at sea that the ship threatened to break up." The poor unsuspecting pagan sailors are petrified and they alternately pray ("each of them called on his own god") as they frenziedly throw overboard all of their precious cargo. Meanwhile, the perpetrator of this unexpected upheaval lies within the ship's hold peacefully asleep! When the captain discovers our friend Jonah in such unconcerned slumber, he is properly outraged. In utter amazement he castigates the prophet: "What do you mean by sleeping? Get up! Call on your god!", little realizing that it is Jonah they should have heaved overboard.

at the Western Wall
Jerusalem

Perhaps it is the look which passes over Jonah's face when mention of his God is made. Perhaps it is the sudden realization on the part of the sailors that Jonah is not one of them. Perhaps it is just a seaborn intuition that this is not nature's storm only. Or perhaps it is Jonah's very act of sleeping — the assumed nonchalance of the imposter trying to be detached from events which will unveil his disguise. Whatever it is, the sailors suddenly know that Jonah is their man.

So the device of the lots is proposed "and the lot fell to Jonah," which by this time is no surprise to anyone. Probably even Jonah perceives that this part of the game is up. Yahweh has outdistanced him.

With simple honesty (the other side of his impulsiveness), Jonah forthrightly declares: "I am a Hebrew, and I worship Yahweh, the God of heaven, who made the sea and the land." He then recounts his flight.

The sailors are agape. The numerous and conflicting emotions which dawn upon each swarthy face border on the comical: utter disbelief, latent anger, total relief, consummate terror, puzzled speculation. And of course, the overwhelming question: "What are we to do with you?" They do not want to die; neither do they want to kill a prophet of Yahweh. For they (pagan though they be) are far more awed and reverential of Jonah's transcendent God than Jonah is. Perhaps familiarity with the divine always contains this darker possibility — a too casual assessment of his will and purpose. At any rate, the seamen hold sacred what the prophet shrugs away: his belonging to Yahweh. So, although Jonah offers them his life in return for tranquility in theirs, they are extremely reluctant to carry out his suggestion: "Take me and throw me into the sea." Instead they row even harder in an attempt to reach the land.

However, it is to no avail. Who can contend with Yahweh and win? And thus, the waters grow more treacherous.

At this point an interesting phenomenon occurs in a pageant already replete with spectacle: the pagans pray to Yahweh, the God whom Jonah has not yet so much as even addressed. "O Yahweh, do not let us perish for taking this man's life; do not hold us guilty of innocent blood; for you, Yahweh, have acted as you have thought right." It is the prayer of desperation uttered in absolute conviction that Yahweh is, indeed, God — almighty and inscrutable in design. Having so prayed, the sailors then act. "And taking hold of Jonah they threw him into the sea." The desired effect prophesied by the runaway himself occurs: "The sea grew calm again." Ironically, it is this climax (for the sailors) which totally converts them. "They offered a sacrifice to Yahweh and made vows."

Jonah probably never knows this, of course. He is too busy floundering around in the sea to think about the effect his prophecy has had on its hearers. He may never realize that the result of his first "long distance run" has been the total conversion of an entire ship. So often the prophetic act bears its fruit unconsciously.

The seamen sail away. Act I is completed. Act II begins: enter the fish.

"Yahweh had arranged that a great fish should be there to swallow Jonah; and Jonah remained in the belly of the fish for three days and three nights."

This time the distance Jonah clocks is more of an internal mileage. Suspended between heaven, earth and Sheol; surrounded by the waters of the nether world; undulating within the frame of one of Yahweh's great sea monsters, Jonah comes to terms with himself. There is nowhere to run. For all he knows, he may be heading towards death or life. This may be his destruction or rebirth. He does not know whether Leviathan is transporting him to bliss or despair. All he knows is that he had better pray. And so he does, with complete openness and humility, aware of his transgression: "Those who serve worthless idols forfeit the grace that was theirs." Jonah perceives the idol he has served; it is himself. Thus, in complete repentance Jonah cries out fervently to Yahweh:

> "But I, with a song of praise,
>   will sacrifice to you,
> The vow I have made, I will fulfill.
> Salvation comes from Yahweh" (Jonah 2:10).

With this ringing declaration, Jonah is forgiven and Yahweh speaks to the fish who delivers our prophet safely to the shore. But Yahweh is not finished yet; nor is Jonah. There is still the initial mission left unfulfilled. Jonah is accountable for what he has not done. And so "the word of Yahweh was addressed a second time to Jonah: 'Up!' . . . 'Go to Nineveh . . . and preach to them as I told you to.'"

Obediently, with great alacrity and immense enthusiasm, Jonah now runs to the great city, shouting out his prophecy: "Only forty days more and Nineveh is going to be destroyed." Swifter than Jonah's feet can carry him, the message is transmitted. "And the people of Nineveh believed in God; they proclaimed a fast and put on sackcloth, from the greatest to the least." Thus, Act II is concluded, for God relents! "He did not inflict on them the disaster which he had threatened." The mission is successful — but Jonah has failed.

The stage is now set for the final act as Jonah unleashes his towering rage.

To Yahweh, the great "arranger," the protagonist in the drama, the director and producer of all cataclysmic events, puny little Jonah must indeed seem comical. In a storm of fury he bellows at Yahweh, castigating him for an assortment of ill-employed stage tricks which ultimately effected (in Jonah's opinion) the wrong denouement. "A God of tenderness and compassion, slow to anger, rich in graciousness, relenting from evil," this is Yahweh who "sold out" his prophet. Jonah will be the joke and ridicule of Nineveh. Costumed in self-righteousness, he has become the drama's buffoon. Tragedy has turned into farce.

In his anger Jonah reveals more than he probably should (the darker side of his impetuosity), as he firmly announces to Yahweh the secret reason lurking behind his first long flight from mission. Jonah is afraid of failure. "Ah! Yahweh, is not this just as I said would happen when I was still at home? That is why I went and fled to Tarshish." Prophetically, Jonah knew that Yahweh's vindication resided in Jonah's failure. For Yahweh to be God in divine terms Jonah had to fail in human ones. Jonah could foresee Yahweh's mercy to believing Nineveh, and he could not bear the humiliation of being an unvindicated prophetic voice. Thus, he ran away and so he wishes to do now. It is his pattern for handling fear, failure, and chagrin. "Yahweh, please take away my life, for I might as well be dead." It is the ultimate request — the last flight to freedom.

Yahweh simply asks the unanswerable question: "Are you right to be angry?" Jonah has no response and so stomps off to sulk.

It is here that we have the inclusion of the grace-note of the play, the little added epilogue which completes the drama. We might call it parabolic of the larger drama for through it Yahweh gently instructs his heartsore, worn-down prophet.

Our scenery now includes a castor-oil plant. "Then Yahweh God arranged that a castor-oil plant should grow up over Jonah to give shade for his head and soothe his ill-humor; Jonah was delighted with the castor-oil plant." He stretches out against it restfully and awaits the hoped-for destruction of Nineveh.

Then "God arranged that a worm should attack the castor-oil plant — and it withered." Jonah becomes slightly distressed.

Finally, "God arranged that there should be a scorching east wind; the sun beat down . . . on Jonah's head." Jonah becomes infuriated. Abandoned outside a city that will not fall, deserted by a plant that will not shade, angered by a sun that will not set, scorched by a wind that will not cease, pursued by a God who will not lose, Jonah psychologically starts to run. "He was overcome and begged for death." Again, Yahweh asks the same basic question: "Are you right to be angry?", angry about the castor-oil plant, about the sun and the wind, about the city of Nineveh, about your own failure? "Are you right to be angry?"

Undaunted (because still enraged) Jonah replies caustically: "I have every right to be angry." It is then that Yahweh answers his prophet with tenderness, graciousness, and compassion — those very characteristics Jonah had formerly deplored.

> "You are only upset about a castor-oil plant which cost you no labor, which you did not make grow, which sprouted in a night and has perished in a night. And am I not to feel sorry for Nineveh, the great city, in which there are more than a hundred and twenty thousand people who cannot tell their right hand from their left, to say nothing of all the animals?" (Jonah 4:10-11).

Thus the drama ends. Yahweh has the last word just as he had the first. Jonah is agape much as those salty sailors were. In the blazing sun, under the peaceful skies of repentant Nineveh, the city not destroyed, Jonah is struck by truth. He had run miles, gone to the depths of the sea, hurled himself against Divinity, proclaimed death and doom, only to find prophecy fulfilled within himself. He is a sign of Yahweh's faithful love — to Jonah! The sailors and the Ninevites are but beneficiaries of Jonah's own conversion. He perceives that all his running has been designed to this one end: that through his unfulfilled prophecy (and accepted human failure) Yahweh's voice of love be heard.

For Yahweh's message is never solely of destruction, terror, or doom. He is never vindicated by storm or fire or death. Only in this one sign can he be irrevocably known: "Salvation comes from Yahweh." This is the prophetic message Jonah learns to speak for he discovers through his failure what salvation really is: being known and loved by Yahweh who is merciful and forgiving. Not a bad lesson for anyone to learn: pagan sailors, decadent city-dwellers, or terrified, angry prophets.

Sitting It Out with Job:
The Human Condition

For a long time now, he had haunted me, this acerbic little man—haunted me and annoyed me. He seemed so utterly sore: ulcerous wounds on the outside, bleeding heart on the inside. Who needed it?

Who also needed his words—thunderous, vehement complaints denouncing life, God, man. Quite honestly, who wanted to tangle with all this writhing agony? It might underscore the already too familiar.

So determinedly, I put him aside and concentrated on other things: the joy of Joseph, the fidelity of Ruth, the trusting surrender of Esther. But they occupied my time, not my mind. For behind them all, there he sat, that angry, implacable figure—stinking, screaming, wildly gesticulating. Ultimately, against my will and better judgment, he antagonized me to his side—flies and all.

To be candid, I hate flies. And odors like disease and manure. And unmitigated complaining. And pseudo-sympathy. It all talks and walks like death. So I didn't really like Job in his utter humanity. It was too graphically prophetic. That was the haunting part. The annoying part is that, in spite of all of it, I stayed.

So now there are two of us sitting in the noonday sun—hot and stubborn and mad. Eventually, someone will have to speak.

"In the end it was Job who broke the silence and cursed the day of his birth" (Job 3:1).

Just like that—for twenty-six verses—spewing out anger. Why was he born? Why couldn't he die? Words filled with dread of the future, sleeplessness, lament.

Grief has a way of doing that, you know. Utter stone . . . then the crack across the surface. A few heaves—abruptly a mountain becomes a volcano, lava of words and emotion searing out everywhere. Shock on the faces of onlookers stampeding to take cover: "Spare us your painful fire, please. *Please.*" While the volcano rages on. And then . . . the deathlike stillness . . . followed by meaningless words trying to make meaning. A survivor gasps:

69

"Eliphaz of Teman spoke next. He said: . . . 'If I were as you are . . .'" (4:1; 5:8). If . . . *if*. Through all the wreckage and debris. . . . "If I were as you are. . . ." *if*. The irony of those words: Who can be like Job, when one is sound and whole and safe, free from loss, darkness, despair? Speaking out of loved ones alive and farm lands intact, what can such a one as Eliphaz know of unanswered questions, heart-rending supplications? For him, do they even exist?

Silence. Then, imperceptibly, a stirring from the ashpit, a flicker of the eyelash. Job speaks:

"If only my misery could be weighed . . . .
    what wonder then if my words are wild?
The arrows of Shaddai stick fast in me,
    my spirit absorbs their poison . . ." (6: 2-4).

Ah yes — those poisonous arrows of Shaddai; those intimations of doom from Sheol that stick deep into the soul; the certain knowledge that never again will there be innocence and joy. And always there are the bitter questions asked over and over of self: *Will I be able to go on? Why go on anyway? Where are my friends? Why can't they understand?* Fear and loneliness. The Underworld.

Someone creeps near to draw out the sting, to touch the cracked skin. It is Bildad. He urges humility:

"You too, if so pure and honest,
    must now seek God, plead with Shaddai" (8:4-5).

These are soothing words indeed: "*If* you are honest." This is an answer with insight! "Seek God, plead with Shaddai." How is Job to do this when Shaddai has disappeared? Where is God to be found for Job, the sufferer?

A lull ensues. The hot breeze blows. Flies buzz. Then a voice. And Job said:

"Your own hands shaped me, modeled me;
    and would you now have second thoughts, and destroy me?" (10:8).

The appeal and bargaining begin. Who hasn't done it? Bargaining with self; bargaining with God. And the panic: how dare oppose the Almighty's will? How dare question Yahweh God Omnipotent? Suppose I am right? What difference would it make? Suppose I am wrong? What then? Yet, what is there to lose when one has already lost everything? "Yahweh, give a little happiness before death." Is this too much to ask? Appeal and bargaining — who hasn't done it?

Zophar apparently. For he queries pontifically:

"Can you claim to grasp the mystery of God,
    to understand the perfection of Shaddai?

It is higher than the heavens: what can you do?
It is deeper than Sheol: what can you know?" (11:7-8)

Truth — unadorned and stark. What can you do? Nothing. What can you know? Nothing — absolutely nothing. That is the darkness, the pain. Helplessness in the face of the abyss — the human condition. What can you know? What can you do? Nothing — nothing except to confront Yahweh. Despair — the human condition.

Then, convoluting tortuously, comes the rush of Job's words, ejaculated with the vehemence of despair, discharged with the agony of futility, resolute like one maddened:

"I mean to remonstrate with God. . . .
Silence! Now I will do the talking,
   whatever may befall me.
I put my flesh between my teeth,
   I take my life in my hands.
Let him kill me if he will . . ." (13:3, 13-15).

The pathos of those words, the frenzy! The "last-chance syndrome." Where have we heard it before? From what corner of the universe has it not cried out? We have heard it on the lips of the dying; in the hearts of survivors; from the tomb called old age and rejection; out of the spectral stare of disease and starvation. Who has not, at some point in life, taken one's flesh in one's hands, remonstrated with God?

But Eliphaz cannot understand. Not yet having plumbed the depths of misery, never having drunk suffering's cup to the dregs, he cannot fathom the pain that would drive a man to contend with God. He only sees the obvious: anger and rebellion. And so he says: "See how passion carries you away!"

Passion — that double-edged sword of grief and joy, the ecstasy and bestiality of man, the most cherished and most despised of gifts. Passion. Who has not longed for its transforming unity? Who has not wept over its fragmented discord? Passion.

I watch him — Job — as he masticates Eliphaz's words. He chews them carefully as one chews a fish with bones. He moves his teeth cautiously around them and just as cautiously his tongue. But he will not swallow them. He holds them in his mouth, in one corner of his cheek, and stares ahead at emptiness. "Swallow them," I plead silently, urgently, "or spit them out. Don't hold them lest they choke you." But there is nothing — only that awful bulbous cheek and the empty stare.

It is mid-afternoon, the height of heat and sun, reason's siesta time. Perspiration drips. Things swim before the eyes: mirages, desert visions, subconscious creatures from the soul. The universe crumples like a folded fan. The breeze pants hot across inert bodies, creating the sense of being played upon, fretted.

And then, heartrendingly Job cries out:

"He has shattered me!
He has pierced me!
He has breached me!
He has borne down on me!
Every fibre of my heart is broken!
I weep! I cry out!
Still he shoots his arrows into me!
I am overcome!"

The Litany of Passion, divine passion. Good old platitudinous Eliphaz has finally hit the mark. Unerringly, unknowingly, Job has been ravished. In the nakedness of a cloudless day, we have seen him vanquished, embraced. He gasps and swallows. The lump travels to his throat and lodges. Is it possible that loss is no longer what he wails? Could it be that he and Yahweh are suddenly bartering for surrender? Without moving an inch, Job has traversed a terrain. I swallow too.

Silence impregnates solitude. No one stirs. The sun moves imperceptibly. A shade begins. Coolness trickles down my brow. I close my eyes and wipe the damp. I feel like sleep. Or death. I feel like dying if dying is so much a pouring out. I feel like sleep if sleep is like release. I feel. . . .

Mournfully into the dusk, Bildad speaks, musing:

"Driven from light into darkness
    he is an exile from the earth" (18:18).

"Driven from light into darkness." Like the sun's course. Like the ocean's tide. Like the season's change. Like life's pattern! Dawn, noon, night. High, ebb, low. Fertility, fall, winter. Birth, life, death. "Driven from light into darkness." Man.

The mood is infectious. Night hedges in. Animal cries echo. And Job takes up the refrain:

". . . God, you must know, is my oppressor,
    and his is the net that closes around me. . . .
    and covered my way with darkness. . . .
My kindred and my friends have all gone away. . . .
    for the hand of God has struck me" (19:6, 8, 14, 21).

"Driven from light into darkness."

And suddenly, like a meteor across the sky, hope flares briefly:

"This I know: that my Avenger lives,
    and he, the Last, will take his stand on earth.
. . . he will set me close to him,
    and from my flesh I shall look on God.
He whom I shall see will take my part:
    these eyes will gaze on him and find him not aloof" (19:25-27).

It is the song of the prisoner, the condemned. It is the avowal of the sick man, dying. It is the prayer of the faithful soul, deserted. "I know that my Avenger lives."

His words fall into the air dropping like snow on velvet, glistening and hushed. The moon rises and clouds over; the stars wink and disappear. It is the inky time of night. Absolute aloneness. Total isolation. Simple breathing is intrusion. And I think: "Enveloped by the darkness, shall we quietly slip away?"

The eternal temptation of friendship: to quietly slip away. Will he even know we're gone, so absorbed is he in pain? Will he even care, since, in fact, we cannot help? Is there any point to vigils when the heart lies already dead? Truly, how far does fidelity go? How deep does commitment bind?

Ironically, Job gives the answer: fidelity is radical. Its presence is an absolute grace; its absence, an absolute sorrow not to be compared. Job has known the calamity of loss, the pain of bereavement, the suffering of illness. Yet, none of these hold the anguish of desertion and infidelity which is the dark night of the soul; the index finger of Yahweh scraping across the heart; the Ruah, his breath, blowing in the memory, tantalizing, near, but indescribably far away. From this void of absolute emptiness, Job laments in prayer:

> "that heavy hand of his drags groans from me.
> If only I knew how to reach him,
>   or how to travel to his dwelling! . . .
> If I go eastward, he is not there;
>   or westward — still I cannot see him.
> If I seek him in the north, he is not to be found,
>   invisible still when I turn to the south. . . .
> For darkness hides me from him,
>   and the gloom veils his presence from me" (23:2-3, 8-9, 17).

This is Psalm 139 prayed backwards. Even in desolation, Job is a good Israelite. And how accurately he speaks. When human friends depart, the grief is great, but who can measure the torment which ensues when God withdraws? "Under cover of darkness, Yahweh, have You, too, slipped away?"

So I sit and wait and rest. The night leaks out drop by drop. Minutes become ages, then cease. It is the hour of desolation, which is timeless. Inevitable.

And Job continued his solemn discourse. He said:
> "Who will bring back to me the months that have gone,
>   and the days when God was my guardian;
> when his lamp shone over my head,
>   and his light was my guide in the darkness? . . .
> I cry to you, and you give me no answer" (29:1-3; 30:20).

How does one deal with that — the silence of non-response, the answer of the void? Does one walk away dejectedly or does one catapult into the abyss? There is death either way.

And thus, Job carefully considers, examines his days and his nights, probes his heartaches and ecstasies, fingers his hopes and his dreams. Is their memory worth silence or speech, retreat or confrontation? And then with a mighty leap, embodying faith and despair Job issues the challenge, directly, forcibly, to God:

> "Who can get me a hearing from God?
> I have had my say, from A to Z; now let Shaddai answer me.
> When my adversary has drafted his writ against me
> I shall wear it on my shoulder,
>   and bind it around my head like a royal turban.
> I will give him an account of every step of my life,
>   and go as boldly as a prince to meet him" (31:35-37).

With this ringing declaration, argumentation ceases; lament is done. "End of the words of Job" (31:40).

A tremulous pause. Terror grips. Awe invades. The earth turns over and I am sick, my senses reeling. Roaring thunder, thickening night. "My God! My God! We are strangling to death. Our words regurgitate." The desert sand flails. I cover my face; I grovel on the earth; I burrow into the dirt.

"Then from the heart of the tempest Yahweh gave Job his answer" . . . (38:1). In fifty-eight questions!

> Job replied to Yahweh:
> "My words have been frivolous; what can I reply?
> I had better lay my finger on my lips" (40:3-4).

God has a way of doing that — giving questions for answers. He has shown himself divine Socratic:

> But Yahweh God called to the man. "Where are you?" (Gen 3:9).
> Yahweh asked Cain, "Where is your brother Abel?" (Gen 4:9).
> But Yahweh asked Abraham, "Why did Sarah laugh . . . ?" (Gen 18:13).
> [And the one who wrestled with Jacob said:]
> "Why do you ask my name?" (Gen 32:29).
> Yahweh answered him [Moses]: "Who makes him dumb or deaf, gives him sight or leaves him blind? Is it not I, Yahweh?" (Exod 4:11-12).

In fact, all through salvation history we have been closing our mouths with our fingers — too late. Job is in good company. I relax and come up for air. And Job gave answer to Yahweh:

> "I know that you are all-powerful:
>   what you conceive, you can perform.
> I am the man who obscured your designs
>   with my empty-headed words.

I have been holding forth on matters I cannot understand,
   on marvels beyond me and my knowledge" (42:2-3).

Humility. Man before the divine. Nature kneeling to transcendence. The mystery of God. And Job replied:

"I retract all I have said,
   and in dust and ashes I repent" (42:6).

The beauty of humanity. Its capacity for enlargement. Its yearning for completeness. Its ability to change.

"I knew you then only by hearsay,
   but now, having seen you with my own eyes . . ." (42:5).

Knowledge of the heart. Contemplation and surrender. Incarnation reversed: man entering into God.

Peace. My pulse resumes. My heart begins to beat. I can see that I am stained. I can see that I can *see!* A mist of rose gathers in the east. A breeze sighs. Or is it Eliphaz?

When Yahweh had said all this to Job, he turned to Eliphaz of Teman. "I burn with anger against you and your two friends," he said, "for not speaking truthfully about me as my servant Job has done. So now find seven bullocks and seven rams, and take them back with you to my servant Job and offer a holocaust for yourselves, while Job, my servant, offers prayers for you. I will listen to him with favor and excuse your folly in not speaking of me properly as my servant Job has done." Eliphaz of Teman, Bildad of Shuah and Zophar of Naamath went away to do as Yahweh had ordered, and Yahweh listened to Job with favor (42:7-9).

So now there are two of us sitting in the morning's dawn, tired, and joyful, and reborn. Someone will have to speak — but no one does. There is only the echo of a deeper silence — the silence of refrain:

"Where were you when I laid the earth's foundations? . . .
Who decided the dimensions of it, do you know? . . .

Have you ever . . . given orders to the morning . . . ?
Have you journeyed . . . to the sources of the sea . . . ?

Which is the way to the home of the light,
   and where does darkness live?

Has the rain a father? . . .
What womb brings forth the ice . . . ?" (38:4, 5, 12, 16, 19, 28, 29)

Riddles. Unsolved riddles. Man, and mystery, and wonder. Pain, and suffering, and death. The human condition. Riddles. Unsolved riddles. And always the eternal unyielding question:

"Do you really want to reverse my judgment,
   and put me in the wrong to put yourself in the right?" (40:8)

I stretch and rise to go. Job never notices. He is wrapt in prayer, I suppose, for Eliphaz, Bildad, and Teman. I shake out my robe, flex my toes inside my sandals. I start across the sand. The dusty road coils away and flows into the sky; the air trembles with the weight of birds; the grasses caress the soil. Love and infinity. Providence and care. The human condition.

I plod on down the road, humming as I go:

"Has the rain a father? . . .
What womb brings forth the ice?"

Salome

Coiling and weaving,
Snakily seething,
  she glides.
With sinuous beauty
In treacherous duty,
  she hides.

Beckoning, leading,
Arousing, receding,
  she moves.
Silky and gleaming,
Men's fantasy dreaming,
  she proves.

Salome of the dance,
Your importunate chance
  has arrived.
Woman yet child,
Already defiled,
  you survive.

Exploited and used,
Caught in a ruse,
  you decree:
Death is the prize
For which your heart sighs:
  "Let it be."

Life is a dance,
A pattern of chance,
  upbeat and down.

Its rhythm can change;
Joy writhe to pain;
    its music can drown.

So why should you care,
Caught in the snare
    of mother's outrage?
Young and desired,
Spoiled and conspired,
    you gauge

That beauty is power
Which most men devour
    as dole.
In lust each one renders
What love never surrenders —
    his soul.

So take it as yours,
Since bloodletting assures
    you have come of age;
The Baptist is doomed
    (though already entombed)
    and you turn the page

Of a musical score
As you weave round the floor
    with provocative limb;
The piece has been played;
The orchestra paid,
    and you hear the din:

Applause and delight!
What a marvelous sight!
    A girl like a flame,
Bearing a platter
    (indelicate matter)
    a head somewhat maimed.

Salome of the dance,
Your infamous chance
    is complete.
Forever you glide

Captive and tied
   to its beat.

Obedient daughter,
Your steps never falter
   the intricate tune.
For over your shoulder
A woman much older
   dances in gloom.

Ah daughter! Ah mother!
Each is the other,
   wretched and pained.
And down through the ages,
This duo still rages,
   aching and strained.

For what blade can sever
Once and forever
   the umbilical thread?
And what daughter alter
What mother has taught her—
   in dance steps has led?

Salome of the dance
Victim enhanced
Child of the womb,
Over your shoulder
A woman much older
Choreographs doom.

Baptism of Jesus
Church of St. John the Baptist
Ein Karem

In Process: John the Baptist

"Are you the one who is to come, or must we wait for someone else?" (Luke 7:19-20)

It seems that John the Baptist spent his whole life waiting. As such, he was an extremely patient man. Somehow, through the centuries, though, we came to have his story wrong and tend to name him solely as messenger and prophet. In doing so, we miss the mighty impact of his *questions* and the overwhelming witness value of the answers he accepted.

He must have learned something vital — early on — in the womb, as he expectantly waited for the moment of his birth. Again, we tend to ascribe that birth to a certain day and hour when "the time of fulfillment came for Elizabeth to have her child." Actually, it happened earlier, some three months past, when John first met Jesus and greeted him with joy. The symbolism of that encounter must have haunted the heart of John even as its vestiges traced a pattern through the years.

In the darkness of confinement John felt divine intrusion, and in a mystical leap of faith he assented to vocation. And then divinity withdrew and John was left to wait.

Had he known that waiting period was to be not months, but years, he may not have had the courage. Had he known it would end in another dark confinement and another mystical leap to another divine intrusion, he may not have had the strength. But Yahweh was merciful and John was content to grow. And he did so slowly through the years, in the shadow of the question: "What will this child turn out to be?" Neighbors asked it first, but its overwhelming import must have gradually fashioned the contours of his life, drawing him like a lodestone into the current of salvific process.

Surely, in the desert, it must have echoed in the wind and the force of its persistence must have, at times, lured John to fear. "Suppose it is all myth? Suppose I am only a deranged desert man, waiting for a prophecy never to be sent, waiting for a mission never to be given? Suppose I am to be like the shifting desert sand — blown back and forth relentlessly by an overwhelming passion? Suppose I am deluded and my life is just a waste?"

81

What impels a man to wait in the face of such a doubt? What causes him to stand expectant and receptive? What constitutes the tenacious resilience of his heart?

Perhaps it was only the glimmer of remembrance, the flash of light and grace that had exploded in his soul the day his cousin first had come. Who knows the value we posit in the memories of love? Or the power they have to summon us?

So John was summoned, probably in much the same elusive fashion that he had been beckoned all along: a change of mood, a passing desert flower, the way a bird called, the different shape of sky — and suddenly he knew the time had come, and he was ready.

"And so it was that John the Baptist appeared . . . proclaiming a baptism of repentance . . ." (Mark 1:4-5).

This is where we get things all confused. This is where we miss the prophetic message. We are so used to reading all that John *announced* that we never get to discerning all that John was asking.

You see, he lived in much the same condition that we do — waiting for a Someone who is to come. And he did not know any more than we, when that Someone would emerge nor how he could be known.

And so, the discipline of his river days was as intense and all embracing as the discipline of his wilderness. Nothing much had changed except that life was less his own. What *had* shifted was responsibility. Now he was empowered to convert and to baptize and this authority made him responsible for the followers he engendered.

So that is why we find him sometimes a bit harsh — loud and somewhat strident, demanding and even fearsome. He was impelled to trumpeting because he was so needy. And the quality of his message derived from solitary waiting.

The gospel tells us that "a feeling of expectancy had grown among the people . . ." (Luke 3:15). How much more so had it grown within the heart of John?

The anguish of that wait must have been unbearable. "Is this the day? Is that the Man? Am I where I should be? What if he never comes? And why do all these people think I may be he? Am I?"

We will never know the terrible questions John kept buried in his heart, but his flailing words indicate their power and their pain.

"Brood of vipers, who warned you to fly from the retribution that is coming? . . . even now the ax is laid to the roots of the trees, so that any tree which fails to produce good fruit will be cut down and thrown on the fire" (Luke 3:7-9).

And the flame of his own vigilant spirit burned without being consumed.

Then, one day, *he* came. Suddenly, out of nowhere, he strode across the hills and asked for baptism. The relief which floods John is almost pathetic in expression. The force of vindication overwhelms him and in torrential words he iterates:

> "This is the one I spoke of when I said: A man is coming after me who ranks before me because he existed before me. I did not know him myself, and yet it was to reveal him to Israel that I came baptizing with water." . . . "I saw the Spirit coming down on him from heaven like a dove and resting on him. I did not know him myself, but he who sent me to baptize with water had said to me, 'The man on whom you see the Spirit come down and rest is the one who is going to baptize with the Holy Spirit.' Yes, I have seen and I am the witness that he is the Chosen One of God" (John 1:30-34).

The phrases are haunting: "I did not know him myself, and yet it was to reveal him to Israel that I came baptizing with water. . . . I did not know him myself . . . and yet I am the witness that he is the Chosen One of God."

John does not verbalize the implied question but it resides: "*Why* did I not know him? *Shouldn't* I have known him? How could I be asked to witness within such total darkness?

His only uttered protest, however, is humble simplicity: "It is I who need baptism from you . . . and yet you come to me" (Matt 3:14-15).

His only answer received is to "Leave it like this for the time being; it is fitting that we should, in this way, do all that righteousness demands." It is another womb experience: in darkness John feels the divine intrusion and in a mystical leap of faith, he assents to his vocation. And then divinity withdraws and John is left to wait — "for all that righteousness demands."

Certainly, if John had little foreknowledge of preceding events, he has even less concerning those to come. His mission apparently is fulfilled; his prophecy is verified; his baptism is authenticated. What more is there to do? For what does he still wait? What yet will "righteousness demand"?

And then in mounting disbelief, John begins to see the route — the winding way he must tread after straightening other roads; the rough trail he must walk after smoothing other paths. He never asks the question "What will become of me?" He merely waits for it to be fulfilled. The womb, the wilderness, and the river will meet within the prison. Sensing this, John begins divesting.

What a lonely figure he becomes etched against the hills — hand outstretched, finger pointing towards that elusive Someone. "Look, there is the Lamb of God," he urges his disciples — and watches as they walk away to follow a greater prophet. Even when some faithful friends balk at such diminishment, John refuses consolation and speaks of growing smaller.

It is his life played backwards to confinement. It is the full cycle of seed and flower and seed. Cynics choose to call it the terminus of life. Some others, more graced, name it a beginning. All that John perceives is that, again, he lies in readiness, awaiting a delivery. Deep within the bowels of the earth, he languishes in prison, formulating the tormented question that rings across the ages: "Are you the one who is to come or have we to wait for someone else?"

It is a valid death cry. A man should know, shouldn't he, the reason for which he dies? If angering kings on moral issues involves the risk of life, shouldn't one be assuaged in knowing the risk to be well taken?

And so John awaits an answer from his removed and distant cousin — some sort of vindication for the truth that he has uttered. It is a lonely wait made lonelier by the answer:

> "Go back and tell John what you have seen and heard: the blind see again, the lame walk, lepers are cleansed, and the deaf hear; the dead are raised to life, the Good News is proclaimed to the poor and happy is the man who does not lose faith in me" (Luke 7:22-23).

Jesus tells John nothing more than that he is to wait — to wait and see the signs fulfilled — signs which John foretold. He sends this message knowing well that John will never behold any of that for which he preached and for which he will give his life.

And with an utter emptiness, John accepts the answer, urged to a fidelity of heart ratified in faith.

The rest is just the spectacle — bringing all things to fulfillment — "all that righteousness demands." Thus, in one sense, John's life ends whimsically, of no account or importance weighed against a girlish dance. And yet, in another sense, it ends with abrupt savagery, brutal and unpredictable as a woman's rage.

In the darkness of confinement John feels divine intrusion, and in a mystical leap of faith he assents to his vocation. And then divinity withdraws and John is left to wait — to wait for his disciples to place him in the earth.

And so, he does not hear, of course, the tribute he is paid: "I tell you, of all the children born of women, there is no one greater than John" (Luke 7:28). For he is still awaiting the ultimate birth, when Jesus the Messiah will deliver him from death.

His life is prophetic, not because of what he said, but because of how he lived. The irony is that he did not know this. He was a man in process, with a heart full of questions, with a tongue full of words, with a head full of visions. He could never quite integrate the visions and the questions and the words because he lived in mystery. All he could do was wait — wait in silence and darkness and faith — for the words to be uttered, for the questions to be answered, for the vision to be fulfilled.

And in this he is our brother — and very near to us.

Woman at the Well

Strangers; bucket; well.
  Down deep draughts of truth, whetted—
  "Could he be the Christ?"

Of Symbols and Symbolists

"To those who prove victorious, I will give the hidden manna and a white stone —a stone with a new name written on it . . ." (Rev 2:17).

Jesus was a profound and simple symbolist. Amid a plethora of possible transcendent signs, he employed the common tangibles of life to translate and reveal his supernatural origin. Temporal phenomena such as a wheat grain and bread, branches and a vine, sheep and a shepherd, roadways and a gate, light and a tomb, assume eschatological significance in relation to himself.

John, the beloved disciple, whose Gospel narrates the unfolding of these symbols, is not unlike his Master. For in the book of Revelation amid jeweled cities and glittering lampstands, John speaks of a simple white stone as embodying the plenitude of spiritual destiny.

Perhaps there is a link between the symbols of Jesus and the symbol of John. Perhaps our ecstatic reception of the latter (the white stone) is dependent on our faithful interiorization of the former (the symbols of Jesus). For might not the white stone be, in essence, the keystone, capstone, or cornerstone of the total Christian endeavor? Might it not define us infinitely as we have defined ourselves finitely in relation to Christ?

If this is so, then we are compelled by the integrity of Jesus to discover our own integrity in him and thus to uncover our true spiritual selves.

In St. John's Gospel, when interrogated pharisaically as to his origin and testimony, Jesus replies: "I know where I came from and where I am going; but you do not know" (8:14). It is precisely this situation—lack of spiritual knowledge of Christ and lack of spiritual knowledge of themselves *in relation* to Christ—which is the self-imposed curse of the Pharisees. Because they lack identity in him, they lack final and infinite identity in his Kingdom. Instead of his becoming for them a way to the white stone (their spiritual name and identity) the Pharisees convert Christ into a stumbling block—a sign of contradiction. And so he names them hypocrites because they refuse salvation.

Are we any different or any less blind than they? Or do we, too, clamor for proof of identity when confronted with the presence of The One Who Is?

Jesus was also a profound and simple *teacher*. On this much-discussed topic of spiritual identity, he was masterful; he gave his life as a norm. Seven distinct times in John's Gospel, Jesus delineates the pattern for discovering oneself. While the symbols vary, the message remains the same. Ultimately, there is only one way: *his*.

THE "I AM" PASSAGES

The "I am" passages of Jesus provide copious material for reflection — reflection on who he is and on who we are meant to become in him. All seven passages contain the same nucleus developed in a different form. Essentially, in each "I am" section, Jesus provides a symbol for himself, speaks of his personal immersion in the Father, tells us that such self-immolation is freedom, and that in such freedom resides the truth of oneself. In other words, we find the truth of our spiritual identity as Jesus did: by a total and free self-surrender to the Father's will.

The formula is not complex; neither is its implementation easy. The "I am" passages reveal the depth and extent one must go to grow to full spiritual integrity.

Bread

The first way one grows is to be ground down for others. "I am the bread of life," Jesus states (John 6:35). He then tells us that anyone whose life becomes bread for others must expect to be as he is: sustenance-giving, nourishing, consumed. Jesus finds the courage and strength to be so immolated in the freedom of his surrender to his father. "I have come from heaven, not to do my own will, but to do the will of the one who sent me" (6:38). If the Father's will for us is that we also become spiritual food for others, then our personal nourishment cannot be different from Christ's: immersion in the Father. That is the essential truth that Jesus proclaims: "To hear the teaching of the Father and learn from it, is to come to me" (6:45). He, the "Bread of Life," becomes sustenance for us, so that we might sustain others on their pilgrimage to the Father. One facet of spiritual identity, then, is that we forget ourselves to nourish others along the way.

Light

Part of the nourishment entails the support we give to others through a clear and enlightened vision. "I am the light of the world," Jesus proclaims (John 8:12). He also tells us how that light is to be reflected within society: through sound and wise spiritual judgments. Jesus assures us that *his* judgment is sound because he is not alone: "the one who sent me is with me"

(8:16). He further states that the one who sent him is truthful and that "what I have learned from him I declare to the world" (8:26). If one is to become a twentieth-century lamp for an increasingly darkened cosmos, then this characteristic of Christ must be evident: the lucid proclamation of his message. Jesus guaranteed such authenticity when he promised us: "If you make my word your home, you will indeed be my disciples. You will learn the truth and the truth shall make you free" (8:31-32). Part of the identifying mark of a disciple, therefore, is the translucence with which he shines and the transparency through which he allows Christ to shine through him. One who is a light freely guides others through the dark by the clarity of his message and the fire of his vision — a message and a vision which is Father-centered and Christ-revealing.

Gate

The primary manner in which Christ revealed himself was in the tender care he manifested toward others. "I am the gate of the sheepfold," Jesus cries (John 10:7), and how beautifully he describes the role and mark of one whose spiritual identity embodies this symbol: "Anyone who enters through me will be safe: he will go freely in and out and be sure of finding pasture" (10:9). If we are to be "gates" also, gates which allow free access to Christ, gates through which those entering discover the safety and security of his pasture, then we must be ready to be used. It is not easy to be a gate, anymore than it is painless to be bread or light. Bread is eaten; light penetrates gloom; a gate can be broken, battered, abused — forced, and often forgotten after use. But Jesus gave us the one rationale for allowing ourselves to become his signs along the way: "I have come so that they may have life and have it to the full" (10:10).

Shepherd

To give spiritual life to another is the only possible reason one would aspire to the fourth "I am" symbol: "the good shepherd . . . who lays down his life for his sheep" (John 10:11). There are many ways of "laying down one's life" prior to the final physical immolation. And oftentimes it is these less dramatic modes of dying which are so demanding and therefore so neglected. Jesus tells us that the identifying mark of a good shepherd is concern. And concern can be an exhausting quality to possess, for it consumes one in constant care for others. Concern irrevocably removes us from the luxury of self-indulgent detachment. When the "wolves" of trouble, pain, or loneliness attack, the concerned shepherd and disciple, spiritually identified with Christ, remains steadfast with those beset. He can do so for the same reason that Jesus was able to — because he is assured that "the Father loves me" (10:17). It is this certainty in the life of Christ of the Father's love for him that gives Jesus the strength freely to lay down his life for others.

and love.
"Virgin most faithful"

And so I grew up poor,
    bereft of the sure door
    that opens unto Christ.
"Gate of heaven"

And had to search my way to him
    alone,
        unknown —
    by dint of his magnetic will
    that drew me still,
    although I often erred.
"Mother of Our Redeemer"

Now those days have ceased.
My youth is fled.
And all the halcyon time
    of girlish dreams
    is dead and buried
    in a life increased
    (as most lives are)
        with worry
            growth
            and pain.
"Queen of All Saints"

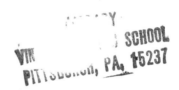

So once again, midstream,
    I ruminate
and claim I seem to know you better,
not through the letter of your person
    but its spirit.
"Spiritual vessel"

For I too, now, am woman
    human
being on the journey
towards the journey's end.
Needing inner peace, release,
    surcease from fragmentation.
"Virgin most powerful"

I too know lamentation —
   have wept for one I love:
   broken, breathless, done.
Have cradled in my arms
   not Son but father
     (god to me).
Have sought out bitterly
    the reason
   for our treason death.
And have received no word.
"Comforter of the afflicted"

Only the "Fiat" that was yours
   sustains me;
Claims me for a life more richly graced
   because more deeply laced
   with struggle,
   heartache,
   faith.
"Ark of the Covenant"

Have found within my battered soul
   a quiet wholesome center
   where I enter
    reverent, hushed
   to pray your song of healing trust
    "Be it done."
"Health of the sick"

Have learned the feeling of the conflict
   known in self-surrender;
Have yearned to render, consummate
   that part of me insensate and unsaved.
"Mother of Divine Grace"

Have reflected on your solitude
   (keeping all things in your heart);
Your loneliness;
Your willingness to share a deeper part
   of his salvific plan —
Your grand and simple eloquence of life
   lived poorly and in strife
   but with much joy.
"Cause of our rejoicing"

And have at last begun to know your past
   in all my present;
Your truth in all my search;
Your birth in this, my dying will,
   that still converts to him.
"O Queen conceived without original sin"
   Gather me in:
      to the ecstasy
         of prophets, virgins, saints;
      to the victory
         that sick and sinful creatures celebrate;
      to the rapture
         of patriarchs, angels, and the martyred dead;
      to the blessedness
         of knowing their Source and Fountainhead.
"Holy Mother of God"